# The Collected Yaps of
# the Wee Ginger Dug
# Volume 4

## By Paul Kavanagh

Wee Ginger Dug Books

Published in 2016 by Wee Ginger Dug Books


Copyright ©Paul Kavanagh 2016

ISBN 978-0-9934057-5-4

A CIP catalogue copy of this book can be found in the
British Library and the National Library of Scotland.


Cover art by Maurice Rapallini

## Dedication

*To Freya and Rhiannon,*

*whose joy in life and search for new experiences are my reasons to keep going.*

# INTRODUCTION

This is the fourth volume of collected articles which were originally published on the Wee Ginger Dug blog, one of Scotland's leading political websites. The Wee Ginger Dug takes an acerbic and caustic look at Scottish politics, based on the principle that we need more mockery in Scottish politics because we have so much to mock.

This volume covers the period around the 2015 Westminster General Election when the national awakening that refused to go back to sleep sought its revenge on a Labour party that had abandoned its traditional supporters in working class Scottish communities.

**Thank God That's Over**

*8 April 2015*

Oh God. Am I a sucker for punishment. Am I in fact a masochist? Maybe I should spend my evenings dripping melted candle wax onto my nipples instead of watching these bloody debates. It would be less painful and probably more productive, and it might even improve my chances of finding a date even if it was one of the 50 shades of grey variety, instead of being stuck indoors having no life and watching bleedin' leaders' debates. Oh God.

Seemingly this debate isn't going out live, despite the BBC announcing it would be live. This gives the BBC plenty of time to edit out any false moustaches and heckling women wearing a dead sheep as a waistcoat, which are generally the only interesting things about these affairs. It also gives time to add the laugh track.

Contrary to suspicious mutterings on social media, the delay is not at the behest of MI5, or even the Scottish accounting unit of the Labour party, it's not even in case Patrick Harvie calls David Coburn a racist twankmonkey - which would only be fair and entirely reasonable - it's all down to the BBC keeching itself in case any audience members heckle that that BBC is biased crap and demand Ken MacQuarrie's head on a plate. The BBC did this during the independence referendum with their "Big Debate" with 16 and 17 year olds. That was shite too. This doesn't bode well.

The debate hasn't even started and I'm bored already. This is shaping up to be one of those shouty and uniforming "Let's disengage the punters from politics programmes" which Scottish broadcasters do so well. This time it's the same four suspects as last night, but with added greenery from Patrick Harvie and purplish populist apoplexy courtesy of UKIP's David Coburn, otherwise known as Jibberjabber the Hutt. I strongly suspect that Coburn is a masochist, after all he belongs to a party that wants to slash the Scottish budget and send our public services back to the stone age. He loves it when Nigel is strict. I can sense a theme for this blog post developing already.

After last night's starring appearance from False Moustache Guy, the only way the party leaders can recover the initiative tonight would be to appear dressed as the cast of the Rocky Horror Show. Jim Murphy BA Politics (failed) has a natural advantage there, what with being a horror show all by himself, although the sight of Jim in a basque and fishnet stockings would probably make an entire nation rush off and drip melted candle wax on their nipples in an effort to purge the image from their minds. Still, it might suit him better than a Scotland strip, and it would certainly be a whole lot more believable than his claims to be a socialist. Rumour has it that chiropodists' clinics all over Scotland were packed out today by people begging for their toes to be straightened after watching Jim last night.

2

Turned BBC1 on ready for the debate. Masterchef is still on. Oh My God, it's False Moustache Man with pan fried gnocchi!

Right, here we go. At last. It's going to be shouty. There are rumours that David Coburn goes off in a huff after someone pan fried his doughy balls. We can but hope.

First question - is it responsible to spend our way out of debt. Jim's up first, looking starey. His eyebrows are running riot and he's only just started. He's promising to end austerity by not undoing anything in George Osborne's budget. Has Jim cleared this with Ed Balls?

Nicola points out that the austerity programme has failed even on its own terms. Austerity has pushed a million children into poverty. Good answer from Nicola.

Ruth claims we're the fastest growing economy. Are we? Is that an actual fact or is that a Ruthie fact? Wullie says austerity is working.

David Coburn calls Alicsammin terrifying. He can do that because he doesn't have any mirrors in his house. He says he wants to keep Barnett but that Alicsammin wants to abolish the Barnett formula and he's the leader of the SNP. An audience member points out Nigel Farage said on the telly today that he wanted to abolish it. David Coburn is a moron, it's official.

Nicola says if we try to spend too much time looking for consistency in UKIP's answers we'll never get anywhere at all. So she sticks the boot into Ruthie instead. Gets cheer from audience.

They're all shouting over one another now. Jim says he just wants to be honest. Well there's a first. And they're all shouting over the top of one another again.

Why does David Coburn sound like a toad? He wants to stop foreign aid. It's all the fault of foreigners. He gets booed. Patrick Harvie says Coburn wants to cancel Britain's membership of the civilised world. He points out that every person on that stage could and should pay more in tax. He'd like to see a Scandinavian approach to both taxes and public services. When Patrick's being honest you can be sure he's honest. This is what distinguishes him from Jim. That and the absence of mad staring eyes and incontinent eyebrows.

Nicola says she wants to end austerity so we can invest in industries and grow the economy. Then there's some shouting about Full Fiscal Autonomy and I'm none the wiser. Jim Murphy says we don't need Full Fiscal Autonomy because we can tax rich houses in London. Scotland's too wee and too poor. This debate is turning into a rerun of the BBC's independence referendum debates.

The Unionists are going on about the state pension now and how it needs to be protected. None of them are pointing out that the UK has one of the lowest state pensions in Europe. Not much protection there then is there.

Nicola points out that Scotland is not a petro-economy. Even without the oil our GDP is the same as the rest of the UK's. This is about taking responsibility for our own resources and our own economy. She's on fire here.

4

Someone brings up fracking. I'm not sure who over all the shoutiness. Jim says that local communities should decide on fracking. This is the man whose party didn't vote for a moratorium on fracking. Now he's changed the subject and he's going back to FFA. His eyes are still staring.

This feels like we're in an independence referendum debate. All shoutiness and screaming, heat and no light. Seems the Unionist parties just can't accept that they won that vote and move on. It's like Unionist groundhog day.

An audience member asks what the panellists can't compromise on. Patrick Harvie says he could never support the renewal of nuclear weapons. He can't support the demonisation of the poor. He makes a call for a new and better electoral system. Coalitions, he says, don't need to be as dishonest as the one we had for the past five years. Scotland deserves a genuine multiparty democracy.

Wee Wullie Rennie gets asked. He says he'll only support nice things. Good things. Fluffy things. Like bunnies, and kittens, and ickle chicks, and better bus services to Kelty. Is there a point to Wullie Rennie? Does anyone know?

Ruthie says she won't compromise on anything that will put the union at risk. She's still fighting last year's campaign. She demands that Nicola will rule out another referendum forever and a day, which is like asking her to give the Unionist parties carte blanche to break all the promises they made during the independence referendum campaign that they've not got around to breaking yet.

Nicola says that she's not even thought about the 2016 manifesto but she'll only consider another referendum if there is a material change in circumstances. But the basic issue is that the people decide, not politicians.

Jim comes out with one of his rehearsed soundbites. He name-checks the Daily Record. James Cook asks him if he remembers what the question is. Jim doesn't. He's too busy trying not to blink. Apart from the red tie he looks like an undertaker. Which is in fact not that far from the truth, Jim's burying the Labour party.

Nicola says that she wants an end to austerity and promises that the SNP will never ever vote for the renewal of Trident. Ruth demands clarification, would the SNP vote against or just abstain? Nicola says they'll vote against - is that clear enough for you Ruth?

This is all very shouty. It's hard to keep up. Even the moderator is shouty. I thought he was supposed to be keeping the rest of them in check and not adding to it?

David Coburn's red line is Europe, surprise surprise. His red line is any compromise with separatism. Nicola says she's really very pleased about that. My god the man is thick. He starts to go on about immigration depressing wages.

Jim Murphy demands that Coburn stops demonising people. Which is a bit rich coming from Jim Murphy, but there ye go. It's still all very shouty.

Nicola says the most depressing thing about the evening is the xenophobic attitude of Coburn, he's a disgrace. Gets a big cheer for that. Not just from the audience but from me as well.

Well that was rubbish. No clear winners there was far too much shouting. But David Coburn was the clear loser, and we can all be grateful for that.

Still, thank god that's over.

## Where No One Has Heard of Google

*10 April 2015*

An opinion poll was published on Thursday night which, astonishingly, showed that the SNP are polling more than Labour, the Tories and the Lib Dems combined. Fully 41% of people who voted Labour in 2010 plan to vote SNP this time. So that fight-back strategy of James Francis Murphy BA Politics (failed) of re-running the independence referendum campaign is really working - for the SNP. Ed Miliband is at it again today, rushing up to Edinburgh in a doomed attempt to shore up the crumbling support for his party by warning Scotland we're too poor for devo max.

This isn't an independence referendum, and telling Scots repeatedly that Scotland is too poor and too weak for Full Fiscal Autonomy just makes voters wonder whose fault that is then. Let's see. Oh yes, that would be the fault of the Unionist parties for taking a country like Scotland, blessed as it is with political stability, situated in a quiet and peaceful part of the globe, with its long tradition of democracy, its educated population, and its embarrassment of natural resources, and turning it into a basket case that can't pay its own way in the world.

Talking of basket cases, I got a letter from Magrit Curran. This is the third or fourth piece of electioneering bumph I've had from the Labour party since the election campaign began, and every single one of them arrived courtesy of the Royal Mail. Must be costing Labour a fortune in postage, but then they don't have any volunteers to deliver anything for them.

To be more exact, it wasn't me who got the letter, the woman who used to live in my flat before I bought it got a letter from Magrit Curran. It's highly unlikely that Magrit is going to write to me, what with me being marked down on her mail-out software as an evil ranting cybernat. Which is fair enough. It's a bit like when they used to mark houses where plague sufferers live, Labour's election mail-out software marks houses where the inhabitants have come down with the virus of nationalism. They mark us with a cross that's joined at the bottom just like an SNP logo, which is unfair, since some of us are Green or SSP voters who're only voting SNP tactically in order give Magrit and her pals the kicking they well and truly deserve.

Anyway, it was very nice of Magrit to write to the woman who used to live in my flat, even though she moved out over six months ago. Not very up to date this Labour software is it, although since the party is still fighting the referendum campaign I don't suppose they felt much need to update it. Sadly for Magrit, I can tell her that the woman who used to live in my flat will not be voting for her. I have no idea how she plans to vote, nor indeed whether she plans to vote at all, but I do know that she no longer lives in Magrit's constituency. So that just leaves me Magrit, and I already bear the curse of

Caledonian separatist Satanism -but the only demon which is going to be exorcised will be her.

Since the letter wasn't a proper stuck down envelopy sort of letter, I read it even though it wasn't addressed to me. I don't think the woman who used to live in my flat would mind too much, since Magrit's letter is of an impersonal nature. A bit like Magrit herself, come to think of it. It's the kind of marketing letter you'd send to people who probably would believe it was butter, even though what Magrit has on offer is very obviously devoid of all nutritional value. Strangely for someone who boasts of the jobs she's brought to the East End of Glasgow, her leafletty letter was printed in Cardiff. So not printing jobs then.

It's funny how a few months changes everything with Labour. During the independence referendum I distinctly recall Magrit and her pals tells us vehemently that warnings that the Tories were a clear and present danger to the NHS were scaremongering of the worst kind. Yet plastered over the back of Magrit's letter is a warning that the "Tories have extreme plans for spending cuts to our NHS". And yes, it's true that they do, but Magrit is hoping that we've forgotten that she was telling us just a few short months ago that there was nothing to worry about. Now she wants us to believe that she's the best person to challenge the threat that she told us wasn't real.

And there's the largest party lie, again. It's Labour's only line of defence and it's as threadbare and implausible as

10

Jim Murphy's claims to be a socialist who's never been a Unionist.

We get a promise to increase the minimum wage to £8 per hour, although I could swear blind that during the debate the other night Jim Murphy promised to raise it to £8.50. He also promised jam, and free gold bars, and pavements made from diamonds, and weather like Spain's, and all Scottish fitba teams are going to be like Barcelona.

There's also the obligatory photos of, ahem, four ordinary members of the public who may or may not be Labour activists who're giving their vote to Magrit. Although at least one of them is a union official in a union affiliated to the Labour party, another has the same name as one of the people who nominated Magrit when she stood as a candidate in the 2010 election, and a third is seemingly a Labour student activist and campaigner. So probably not the ordinary non-political members of the public that Magrit's leafletty letter would have us believe. Getting an endorsement from a campaigner for your own party is not quite the same as wild public acclamation is it. I don't have a problem with any of them giving their support to Magrit, but a little bit of transparency wouldn't go amiss.

Sadly, it's that lack of transparency that has proven to be Labour's undoing. Magrit is campaigning in an East End where no one has ever heard of Google. That would be in the Scotland that depends on the Daily Record for its information. That's the Scotland that elected Magrit and Jim in 2010, and it passed away during last year's referendum campaign with an electric shock when the country plugged in its laptops, smart phones and i-pads.

We're all cybernats now.

# Attack of the Milibawrph

*11 April 2015*

Scotland was blessed yesterday by a visit from Labour's hydra headed leadership, the three monkeys who hear only evil, see only evil and say only evil. It was another of those invitation only Labour party events which have substituted for public meetings ever since the public abandoned the party in disgust. The SNP leadership goes out into the streets and meets with punters, Labour hides in closed rooms and meets with cameras.

The star of the Labour puppet show was the three podiums of the Milibawrph, which appropriately sounds like a unit of measurement for the sickened revulsion Scotland feels for the Labour party. By May 7 the disgust dial is likely to have been ratcheted up to around 40 Milibawrphs, and they'll lose almost all their seats.

Labour can't make this an election about making the UK a better place, so they're just going to attack the SNP again. I can summarise the contents of the Milibawrph speeches on Friday for you, to save you the bother of reading the news reports. They went like this: SNP SNP bad SNP SNP evil SNP SNP Full Fiscal Autonomy bad SNP pensions scary! SNP SNP bad bad SNP boo! SNP SNP

Nicola Sturgeon evil SNP SNP boo! SNP. Oh, and Jim Murphy made a fitba reference.

The visit came the day after an opinion poll showed that the frantic spinning of the Murph E Coyote was unable to resist the crushing gravity of Scottish opinion, and Labour is now plummeting into a very deep and dark Scottish chasm which it will never claw its way out of no matter what shiny new rocket sled policies they send off for from McTernan's Acme catalogue of Tory inspired spin. Labour politicians who have never before been seen in their constituencies are having to go round the doors and beg for votes. And they're getting the doors slammed in their faces.

This wasn't supposed to happen, just a few short months ago the UK press was full of articles explaining how a politician of Jim's calibre would score goals against the SNP and knock them into the back of the net. The SNP had had it all its own way too long, they said, Labour's talent was all in Westminster but that was about to change with the all-conquering James Francis Murphy BA Politics (failed). He wasn't just going to keep all Labour's seats, he was going to gain some from the Lib Dems. But the Smugurph's softly spoken style of schmoozy bonhomie doesn't have the attraction that the metrocommentariat thought it would, and now they're struggling to explain why one of their football metaphorising big hitters is struggling at the bottom of the third division and looks set to be relegated to the amateur leagues.

Labour have spent the last few months promising various flavours of invisible jam, the vow plus marmalade, more nurses than there are people in the entire country, and constantly repeating the constitutionally illiterate lie that only the largest party can form the next government, Scotland has stopped listening to the Labour party. Scotland can't trust Labour ever again after they cheated on us with the Tories. We were deafened by their lies and their promises last year and revolted by them standing shoulder to shoulder with George Osborne. Like the promise Ed Miliband made that was plastered all over the Daily Record to vote No and he'd introduce Home Rule in the first year of his government. We remember these things, the things Labour has forgotten. And like any relationship, once the trust has gone there's nothing left.

But now the Milibawrph has come to Edinburgh to run through the independence referendum all over again. Forget about choosing what you want Scotland, you're too wee and too poor and too stupid. Vote Labour or your pension will die. Vote Labour or die of cancer. Only this time Labour is telling us why we can't have the things that they promised us during the independence referendum if only we voted No. They can't understand why their message has no traction, but then slippery lies and half-truths delivered by oleaginous sleazeballs never do.

The bull-shitters in the abattoir are screaming for Gordie to intervene and save them from their impending slaughter. He's always intervening, usually for the first time, again and again. He's already intervened in

15

Glasgow East, coming to a secret location to speak before an invited audience of the last Labour party supporters in the birthplace of the party. It hasn't made any difference to Magrit's chances. But Labour can't risk Gordie appearing in front of real people in case they ask him what happened to that Vow he was supposed to be personally supervising and he calls them a bigot. It's much safer to keep him behind locked doors where the public can't upset him with any of that troublesome real world and real life stuff.

Things are now so dire for Labour that the best they can hope for is that tactical voting might save a few of their seats. The same tactical voting might also lead to more Tory MPs in Scotland, but in their blind panic and hatred Labour doesn't care. But there are many in the Labour party who think more Tories would be a price worth paying if it stopped Scotland derailing the cosy stitch up between the main Westminster parties.

The tactical voting campaign is being backed by the Telegraph, that same bastion of journalistic standards that brought up Nickileaks and smeargate. But Labour is so desperate that many of them are happily going along with a Tory backed scheme to sneak a few extra Conservative MPs through the back door of the hole in the back of Labour's head - the one that has lost its buttons.

We're going to get a lot more of this over the new few weeks, and it's likely to get increasingly hysterical. Since we're already at defcon full blown hysteria that doesn't leave much space for the rhetoric to go, but it's still not likely to save the Labour party's sorry arses. Because you don't win back the trust of the public by going back on promises you made just a few months ago.

Labour has already lost this election in Scotland and all the Milibawrphing in the world won't save it.

## Are You Still There Gordon?

*12 April 2015*

I didn't get up to watch the, ahem, debate on the Scottish Politics Show on Sunday morning. It was another of BBC Scotland's sterling efforts to disengage punters from politics. A news announcer on Sky News called it "lively", which is a bit like calling a lynch mob lively. I caught the debate on i-player later in the day. Well I say debate, it was more three Unionist politicians in a tag team throwing buckets of shite at Nicola Sturgeon while Gordon Brewer polished his nails and wondered when it was all going to be over.

Calling it shouty is an unkindness to crazy people who scream delusional madness in the street. Shoutiness at least involves coherent words, sometimes even entire sentences. This was just inchoate screams from the grave that James Frances Murphy BA Politics (failed), the Action Krankie, and Wee Wullie the driver of the Number 17 to Kelty are collectively digging for the Union. And Gordon was happy for them to get on with it, when he wasn't contributing to the screaming himself. At one point Jim Murphy asked him - are you still there Gordon? And he'd have been as well going off and making everyone a nice cup of tea for all the positive benefit he brought to the proceedings.

This is what happens when you start from the default position that politicians deserve respect, when in fact what they really need is to be yelled at - Haw you! Aye you! Ya rude bastert - shut yer geggie or leave the room. A'll no be tellin ye a second time. Which is what I'd have said. And this is why I'll never moderate a rammy on BBC Scotland. The reason our politicians behave so badly is because they are allowed to.

To be fair, Nicola did her share of shouting back, it was either that or drown under the torrent of dementia being poured on her by Jim and Ruth, although she did actually keep quiet at times when it was the others' turns to speak. Something you can't say for Jim Murphy, who brought smug creepiness to an entirely new pitch of demented shouting. It would appear that Jim thinks that high fiving the Tory representative and ganging up with her against the SNP is going to bring disaffected Labour voters back to the fold, and this brings us a lot closer to understanding why he's a BA Politics (failed) and why most of his colleagues are soon going to be ex-MPs. Jim clearly has failed to internalise the fact that it was cosying up to the Tories that has reduced his party to the dire state it's currently in - drowning in an onslaught of odium from ordinary punters.

Meanwhile I discovered, courtesy of a gloriously delusional article from Andrew Gilligan in the Telegraph, that I'm an evil bullying cybernat because I said unkind things about Magrit Curran. Or "Margrit" as the Telegraph puts it, twice. Of course you can't really expect the Telegraph to copy things accurately, or to be familiar with the Glaswegian vernacular, or indeed Scottish politics, and all these instances of ignorance were fully on display in Andrew's article, which was funnier than anything I've ever written. Only he didn't do it on purpose.

Of course I've still got a very long way to go before I reach the dizzying heights of evil cybernatdom achieved by Stu Campbell of Wings over Scotland. Stu Campbell is so evil that even things that haven't happened at all are still his fault. Stu Campbell was on the grassy knoll in Dallas and shot JFK with a kitten he'd infected with ebola and stuffed into a polonium laced teapot. And the kitten was English. True fact that. It will be coming to an SNPout hashtag near you very soon.

Anyway, apparently I'm a prominent SNP supporter. Gosh. I fully intend to put the word "prominent" in large letters on my gay dating profile as it will certainly increase my chances of finding a man to go out with. But the thrust - there's another word I could put on my gay dating profile - of Andrew's piece was to make out that I am part of some organised campaign directed by the SNP. Which is big bollocks. Oh there's another phrase for the profile.

While it is true that I fully intend to vote for the SNP's Natalie McGarry in Glasgow East - because unlike Andrew Gilligan I live there and actually know where Shettleston is and have seen at first-hand how Labour has let it down for generations - I am not a member of the SNP, I do not receive directions, finance, or support from the SNP, and no one in the SNP has ever told me what to write or not to write. And if they ever did I'd tell them bugger off.

It suits the Telegraph's narrative to depict Scottish working class people as sheep who need to be directed and told what to say and do - that's how our Westminster masters see us after all. They are incapable of comprehending the truth - that I'm just an ordinary East End punter who calls things as he sees it, and I don't see anything of merit in Magrit. I don't prevent anyone else speaking. I don't shout down those I oppose politically. I mock, I make fun, I slag off, I flyte. And I refuse to be patronised by morons with an agenda.

But then it's bullying of me to point that out. What's really scary for the Andrew Gilligans of this world is that I am far from being alone. There are thousands of opinionated lippy Scottish people, and we found our voices during the independence referendum. We scare the Telegraph columnists of this world. And we scare politicians who think they have a right to shout over the top of those they disagree with.

I fully intend to keep on scaring them. And I know there are thousands who are doing the same, with wit and with words and with humour. We are all still here, even if Gordon isn't, holding them to account. We rewrote the rules last year. Welcome to the new Scotland.

## All Your Base Are Belong to Us, Jim

*13 April 2015*

James Francis Murphy BA Politics (failed)'s sharply honed political instincts are being borne out. He told us there would be a late surge in Labour's vote, and he's right. There is indeed a late surge in the Labour vote, it's just the surge is in the opposite direction from the one he was hoping for. On Monday another Scottish opinion poll was published, showing that the SNP are on 52%, yes you did read that right, and the Greens on 3%.

That's an increase of 6% in the SNP's vote share, and a corresponding drop of 6% in Labour's. Some projections based on these figures would leave Labour with just two seats in Scotland, neither of which would be Jim Murphy's. Fears and smears end in tears Jim, and now all your base are belong to us.

If this poll is right, then 55% of the Scottish vote is going to pro-independence parties. But evil cybernats and those who would do ill to Wee Dougie Alexander's career shouldn't get too excited. Some of the fieldwork was carried out before the hauf-arsed attempt to smear Nicola as a Tory lover, and all of it was before Sunday's hammy rammy ding dong when Jim Murphy made a complete and utter arse out himself, schmoozed up to the Action Krankie, and pissed off more than half the women in the country and a sizeable chunk of the men. There could be more Scottish surginess yet to come. It looks like Jim's going to be joining Wee Wullie Rennie on the number 17 to Kelty, via Cowdenbeath and terminating in extinction.

Yesterday I saw a wee forlorn group of Labour canvassers. There were four of them, and they didn't look like they were wildly enthusiastic about their task. At least one of them was a local cooncillor. They're hopelessly outnumbered by the SNP canvassers locally, and the official campaign has only just got started. The SNP seem to outnumber Labour on the ground by about ten to one, and this time Labour can't bus supporters up from dahn sarf to boost their numbers.

Also on Monday Labour unveiled its manifesto for the General Election. It was a "let's not scare off potential Tory voters" kind of manifesto. Jim Murphy was hoping that buried somewhere in the fine print there was a wee proviso stating "except for viewers in Scotland", because for the past couple of months he has been telling anyone who would listen that there won't be any cuts in Scotland. We can grow the economy, Jim said, no need for cuts, he said. While slagging off Nicola Sturgeon for saying remarkably similar things.

Unfortunately for Jim Ed Baws rummaged around in his chancellorial bawsbag and stated that Scotland can't be exempt from spending cuts under a Labour government. Jim's leadership of the Scottish accounting unit has been turned into a yolk by his own party leadership.

Being exhausted after his recent media performances, Jim didn't make it to the manifesto launch, all that patronising takes it out of him. It was left to Ed Miliband to look snide instead, which he achieved by imagining he was confronted with a bacon sandwich and a press photographer. Desperate to avoid looking like a suicide bomber with a pointy finger, Ed did his wavy superglued hand thing, and promised voters that he could be as nasty as any Tory could. But he'd do it with a sad face, because Labour's the caring cuts, austerity, and sooking up to bankers' party. The manifesto itself was an exercise in management wankspeak, full of words like synergy, proactive, and going forward into blandness.

Chuka Umunna - Labour's business and pensions spokesperson - was interviewed by the assembled reporters while he was standing in front of a Labour campaign coach plastered in progressive Labour slogans like "Foreigners are bad", and "We promise to look sad when we cut your benefit." Pointedly, with a sharp stick he was poking in the ribs of the Scottish branch office, Chuka tossed a few more eggs at Jim and said, "The leader of the Scottish party will not be in charge of the UK budget."

And if you looked very carefully you could see Jim's legs poking out from beneath the wheels of the bus, along with the splattered hopes of Labour saving its Scottish seats and a pile of broken eggshells.

Clearly, the Labour leadership - that will be the real Labour leadership and not Jim's imaginary branch office variety - have decided that the party in Scotland is a lost cause. They can only lose 41 seats in Scotland, but many more seats are at play in England. Since the only way they can save any seats in Scotland is to adopt policies that will make them lose the support of the Tory press in England, and they crave Tory media approval like an SNPout zoomer craves a smear, Jim gets the off. So Chuka chucks Jim under the battlebus in return for a sympathetic story in the Express about how the Labour candidate in some marginal seat in Toryshireland is distantly related to Princess Di. And order and balance is restored to the universe.

Jim sees Labour's private polling and their canvass returns. This may be the reason for his increasingly hysterical public performances. Jim's day starts with a look at the figures showing his career prospects are plummeting faster than Jackie Baillie in pursuit of an NHS scare story, and that's distressing for him since his career is the only principle he's ever stuck firm to. In fact, it's the only principle he's ever known. It's why he went into politics in the first place. Without his political career Jim has got nothing left. He could try to make folksy railway documentaries like Michael Portillo. But Jim touring the country on an Irn Bru crate batting away eggs with a Bradshaw guide has already been done. Besides, the Caledonian Express has already left the station and left Jim behind, shouting angrily at pensioners.

Jim's assured himself a place in the history books. It's just not the place he wanted. He'll be remembered as the man who killed the Labour party in Scotland, sacrificed on the altar of Jim's career. Only he won't save his career either. All your base are belong to us Jim.

## The Silence of the Bams

*14 April 2015*

Hahahahahahahahahahahahahahahaha ... and breathe ... hahahahahahahahaha. That's been me for the past day and a half. The Murph E Coyote has looked down past his frantically spinning paws and has seen that he's supported by nothing more substantial than the thin air of a BBC Scotland broadcast. Now Jim is plummeting into the canyon and taking the rest of the Labour party in Scotland with him. We're just waiting for the cloud of dust and the satisfying smack of schadenfreude. Never has a political career come to such an embarrassing end since Iain Gray was waylaid by a cheese baguette and the baked goods of the grassroots.

The wheels have come off the Labour battlebus which was being driven by James Francis Murphy BA Politics (failed) yet still the bus has managed run into a ditch and flatten a kitten in the process. The wheels themselves have run Jim over and splattered his career like a hedgehog wearing a vote Labour rosette that took a wee daunner down the M74 into Jimmy Hood's constituency. And that doesn't even begin to describe the multiple flusterclucks which have beset Jim's campaign to save the Labour party in Scotland as a springboard for his career.

A poor week started with the slagathon screaming match which BBC Scotland glorified with the title debate, in which Jim managed to show less self-control than a serial fantasist with chronic diarrhoea and a sensitivity to women's issues last seen in a caveman dragging his trophy wife out of the cave by her hair. It was such a gobsmackingly poor performance that not even the usual suspects could defend it on the interwebbies. And this particular episode has still to be reflected in a Scottish opinion poll. No wonder Kezia Dugdale was looking even more miserable than she usually does.

This was followed by an opinion poll which showed Labour's support is being haemorrhaged more quickly than one of Hannibal Lector's dinner guests. The pro-independence SNP and the Scottish Greens have between them the support of 55%. Oh the delicious irony. Iain Gray was done in by a sandwich, this is Jim's yum yums of democracy.

Despite a near total onslaught of policy initiatives, promises of free jam for everyone, and the dubious claim that the Labour party in Scotland won't implement any cuts, Labour is still losing support. The thing is it doesn't matter what you say, promise or claim, if it comes out of the mouth of a man no one trusts then it's not going to be believed. And no one trusts Jim. No one. A 1970s Radio One DJ at a girl guides' party is more trusted.

And then the last tattered remnants of Jim's trustworthiness were put through a mincer, diced, sliced, freeze dried and pounded into dust then blown out the window by his own party leaders. He was quite pointedly told by the big boys dahn sarf that he doesn't get to say what cuts there will be. That's Ed Baws who gets to decide that. Slap, kapowie, blam.

Jim was so affronted after being slapped about by Ed Baws and fried by Chuckie that he refused to appear on STV's Scotland Tonight. And this is a man who makes the cast members of TOWIE seem camera shy. Instead he had to stay in and wash his rapidly greying hair, at least that part of it which he hasn't torn out yet. It was the silence of the bams. His embarrassment was as terminal as Reporting Scotland story about the NHS. Which is a shame, because his glowing slapped face is the only red thing about him and displaying it might have made some viewers believe his claim to be a socialist, at least those who would also believe that Rylan had written a scientific paper about the application of quantum physics to teeth whitening and that the Large Hadron Collider is actually a tanning shop in Southend on Sea.

Which explains a lot - Jim's the Rylan of politics, all presentation and brain dead content. Although to be fair Rylan does have better hair and teeth. If you take away the hair and teeth there would be nothing left of Rylan at all except a supreme lack of self-awareness. And this is also true of Jim Murphy.

By Tuesday @JimforScotland was trying to get back on his feet, in the same way that a drunk man with his pants round his ankles tries to get back on his feet after falling face first in the gutter. Jim adopted the Twitter handle @JimforScotland in order to persuade the Rylan's of this world that he puts the interests of Scotland first, although a more accurate Twitter handle for him would be @JimforJim. Jim has only ever put Jim's interests first, and that's the reason why he took the gig as branch manager of Labour's Scottish accounting unit in the first place.

Before taking the job, @JimforJim had backed the wrong horse in the Labour leadership race. Jim had pinned his colours to the mast of the wrong Miliband. When the one with the superglued fingers took over, he demoted Jim, who saw that his career prospects were sinking more quickly than Iain Gray doing the breaststroke with a bread stick. @JimforJim decided to take over the Scottish branch of the party, and merrily set about undermining Johann Lamont - although to be fair Johann had long since excavated the basement all by herself - while skanktimoniously preaching that the party needed to be united and calling for people to stop briefing against one another. Except Jim, who was the one doing most of the briefing.

The poor wee sowel believed his own hype. The Scottish press wouldn't subject him to any serious scrutiny, and Jim could then take credit for saving the Scottish party to use it as his own personal power base just like Gordie before him. Then he could launch his own campaign for the Labour leadership after Ed lost the General Election. That's what he really means by @JimforScotland. But the best laid plans of mice and Murphs gang aft agley. Jim has silenced Labour in Scotland forever. The silence of the bams.

Hahahahahahaha ... and breathe ...

## Toad Hall and the Tenants' Buy-Out

*16 April 2015*

The Lib Dems and UKIP launched their manifestos on Wednesday, and nobody in Scotland gave a toss. Nigel Farage is still a bawbag who blames everything on immigrants, and no one agrees with Nick - who blames everything on Alicsammin. Nigel Farage blames quite a few things on Alicsammin too, because Alicsammin is Scottish and Scottish people who don't prioritise being British and bow to the mighty absolute sovereignty of Westminster are just the same as foreigners and immigrants. Plus Scottish people speak funny and so do foreigners and immigrants. David Coburn speaks funny too, but Nigel is quite happy to accept him. That's because Jibberjabber the Hutt croaks a mixture of English and toady.

David Coburn appeared on Scotland Tonight to croak about the UKIP manifesto to Bernard Ponsonby, although it soon transpired that only one of them had actually read and understood the manifesto, and it wasn't Jibberjabber the Hutt. Bernard ate him alive, and that can't be good for the cholesterol levels. Besides, isn't eating amphibians a bit French? That means Bernard is probably an immigrant, and it transpires that in UKIPworld everything is all the fault of immigrants, as well as the SNP. More specifically it's the fault of gay immigrant SNP members with HIV and Muslim names.

The main thing to be extracted from the interview, apart from Coburn's spinal column, was an admission from the croaky one that under UKIP Scotland faces £5 billion in cuts over and above of the austerity cuts we're going to get courtesy of Labour or the Tories. What's going to be cut? Bernard looked very fierce. The toady looked for a rock to crawl under but failed to find one. Immigrants are going to be cut. And Nicola Sturgeon's salary. Apart from that he didn't have a clue, but then he didn't have a clue about anything else either, so this was scarcely a revelation. Eventually he ribbitted that it would be up to the Scottish Government. But it was all the fault of people who don't respect the armed forces, and the SNP, and especially immigrants.

Not being able to blame immigrants, Nick just blames Alicsammin. Do you want Alicsammin to have a seat in the UK cabinet, eh? Eh? Do you? Well do you? Nick asked insistently like a bar drunk who blames all his misfortunes on the fact that the Bullingdon bad boys tied him up, poured a gallon of gut rot down his throat, and forced him to pish in his pants. Because if Alicsammin gets a seat in the cabinet there will be a rain of toads. Poisonous toads, rebellious toads, not toadying toads, and that would be a very bad thing, because it would mean no one would have any need for Nick. Oh how he longs for the 2010 election when he won all those debates and everyone agreed with him.

Alicsammin isn't going to be in the UK cabinet, he'd rather poke his eyes out with a rusty knitting needle than do a Cleggie and take the blame for Labour's shortcomings. This is the difference between a master political strategist and a master debater. Much better to wield the rusty knitting needle from the outside, and use it to jag Labour in the bum to make sure they don't get too comfortable and forget their vows to Scotland. Ach Nick son, if only you'd done that with Davie, you might not be pishing your pants now and Danny Alexander might even not be so odiously unelectable.

Well OK, maybe not that last bit. There is an infinite number of universes in the multiverse, and Danny is odiously unelectable in all of them. There is one alternative universe where Danny is still odiously unelectable, but he does have Blair McDougall and David Coburn as best mates and John McTernan is their wee hanger on. That's a really crappy alternative universe and the other alternative universes prefer to pretend it's not there and never invite it to dinner. There's a petition on change.org to change the laws of physics and abolish it. There's also a petition on change.org to abolish Danny Alexander on the grounds that he is supremely pointless as well as odious. That one has a lot more signatures.

There was more pointless odiosity on display in Glasgow today when Davie Cameron appeared with the Action Krankie in order to launch the Tories' Scottish manifesto. No really, they think people are going to vote for them. In Scotland. We're in alternate universe territory again. Davie has come to warn us that the SNP are in bed with Labour. Labour wants us to believe that the SNP are in bed with the Tories. The Lib Dems want us to think that the SNP are in bed with both parties simultaneously, and UKIP think the SNP are in bed with immigrants.

In the poker game of politics, the Tories have matched Labour's bid of an Ed Bawsbag with a Goveslobber, and will raise it with an Iain Duncan Smith crap sandwich with extra sanctions. Labour are not much fazed by this, since in the odiousness stakes they have a Smugurphy, Anas the hereditary MP for Govan, Magrit, Ian Bayonette Davidson, Tom the Blairite Harris, and the no mark who called Nicola a wee lassie with a tin hat. All the Tories have is an Action Krankie and a solitary MP whose sole contribution to politics is doubling up as a panda impersonator.

No one in Scotland really cares what's in the Scottish Tory manifesto, but for what it's worth, the Tories promise to give Scotland smugness, condescension, and a guarantee of contemptuous dismissal. They're hoping that this will trump Labour's offer, which will be unveiled the morra, because Labour will most likely offer only the smugness and condescension - although to be fair they also have a bucket-load of taking us for granted.

In England and Wales, the Tories also want to extend the right to buy to housing association properties, although so far they've not shown any interest in extending the right to buy to the tenants of those annoying people who appear on BBC daytime property programmes. Since housing is devolved they can't do that in Scotland, although the Scottish electorate do seem quite intent on taking ownership of the House of

Commons. We'll buy out Davie on May 7 when Scotland holds the balance of power in Toad Hall. That's a sitting tenants' buy out that will put the fear of god into all the Unionist parties.

## Please Tell Me This Is the Last One

*16 April 2015*

Oh God, I don't want to sit through this. There are navels to be defluffed, and wet paint that needs to be stared at. This debate is going to be very similar to the last one in at least one major respect, Davie Cameron didn't say anything in that one either. Nick Clegg didn't get invited after Davie Cameron decided he was going to spend the evening washing his hair and combing it carefully to cover up his bald patch. That's because no one agrees with Nick any more.

Anyway, I missed the beginning of the debate, but Nigel Farage still thinks everything is the fault of immigrants. Immigrants and Scottish people. He doesn't know where Hadrian's Wall is. It's not clear why he's so obsessed with it, seeing as how it's both entirely within England and was built by Italian immigrants from the EU.

Ed waffled on a bit, Nicola said - "I don't say there's no difference between Labour and the Tories. I say there's not enough difference ... We want to get rid of the Tories but not replace them with Tory lite." Ouch. That's him telt.

The fag paper between the Tories and Labour was illustrated in the following question, about housing policy. Nicola got a lot of applause for saying that social housing needs to be protected for those who need it.

Ed's not opposed to the right to buy, he just doesn't like the Tory policy because of woo. And costings. And woo. And isn't Davie Cameron a bit slimy. Which is trueish, but wooish. His fingers have a life of their own. It's entirely possible that Ed's fingers could get elected PM but the rest of him not be.

Nigel says everyone is stupid. The panel is stupid and the audience is stupid. No one understands housing policy except him. He's been in business so he knows these things, not like the audience, who are stupid. But Nigel is too stupid to realise that pissing off the audience is not how to win debates. Anyway, it's still all the fault of immigrants. And Hadrian's Wall.

Nicola tells him that in his wee world everything is the fault of immigrants. She slaps him down and tells him tae shut his geggie. This is about protecting the supply of social housing and not throwing money away on building houses that get sold off and become unavailable to people who need them. Nicola is kicking serious ass in this debate.

We're onto Trident now. Nigel likes Trident because it's phallic, like him in his dreams. He doesn't care that it costs a lot of money. Big dicks are priceless, aren't they Nigel.

Nicola, Leanne, and Natalie don't want Trident. Nicla says that this island nation doesn't have a single maritime patrol aircraft. The money would be better spent on conventional defence. And she can think of thousands of things that the £100 billion cost of Trident could be better spent on. Like NHS treatment to remove the superglue from Ed's fingers.

Ed's staring at the camera trying to look sincere. It's not a look he fakes convincingly. I'm still creeped out by it. Ed wants to keep Trident too. Because the world is uncertain and so is he. Ed brings up ISIS. Leanne asks does he really think that Trident defends us from ISIS? Ed says no. Then blames Leanne for bringing up ISIS. Then he admits it was him who brought it up and said he wouldn't press the nuclear button against ISIS. Someone's not really thought this through Ed, and it's not Leanne.

Oooh it's the immigrants question. Nigel will be so happy. First up is Natalie who points out that she herself is an immigrant and like the great majority of immigrants she makes a positive contribution to this country. Nicola makes a plea for the debate not to be driven by the intolerance and prejudice of Nigel and brings up a few facts. Ed's staring at the camera again, making decisively chopping hand gestures and not saying any much at all. Nigel says everyone is ganging up on him and being nasty, it's probably because they're all immigrants. Leanne says, you abuse immigrants and then complain that you're being abused, get you. Slagging off Nigel sounds so great in her accent. I'm starting to develop a crush on Leanne - Leanne hen, this gay man would consider turning for you.

This debate is a whole lot less shouty that the other ones. So all that shouty bad tempered incoherence must be Jim Murphy's fault then. That explains a lot. In the quiet of this debate you could hear the hiss of the last bit of air escaping from Jim's balloon. And now we know how civilised politics can be when they don't have Tories or Jim Murphy in them.

Typical, I write that paragraph and then they get all shouty. More precisely Nigel and Ed get shouty. Nigel points out that that Ed's party introduced privatisation in the NHS. Ed retorts that Nigel wants the UK to have a US style insurance system. The Dimbleby tells them to shut it.

The next question is about what deals or agreements the parties would consider after the election. Nigel says he wants a referendum to get out of the EU, which is a way of saying that he'll back the Tories.

Nicola says the most important deal for her is a deal with the Scottish people to make sure our voices are heard in Westminster. And she will never ever do a deal with the Tories. She wants Ed to replace the Tories with something different, something better. If he's prepared to be better, she's prepared to work with him. Leanne and Natalie say the same. Go girls! Get yer act together Ed. People want progressive change, they want fairness, they want justice. Labour won't deliver that if it gets a majority. Labour needs three women to hold it to account.

Ed tries to distance himself. He's got fundamental disagreements with Nicola because she wants to break up the country. He's appealing to Tory voters, just like Labour has always done.

Nicola says she doesn't know what he's talking about. The referendum was last year. This is about getting shot of the Tories. This is an opportunity to deliver an alternative to austerity. Let's deliver real change, not pretend change. Ed comes back with the biggest party lie. Nicola demands he says that he will commit to an anti-Tory bloc. Ed won't and with that puts a final nail into Jim Murphy's coffin. Nicola says - don't turn your back on a chance to kick David Cameron out - and gets a big cheer.

Nicola has owned this debate. There were four big losers tonight, Nigel and three who weren't even there. Davie Cameron, Nick Clegg - and Jim Murphy has lost it big time, stabbed in the back and hung out to dry by his own party leader.

## Jim Murphy, Still Big in Japan

*17 April 2015*

We're surrounded by morons. It's official, it's in the newspapers and on the telly. Or rather, it is the newspapers and the telly. They're morons, idiots, fools, balloons, numpties, muppets, clowns, dumb as soup, thick as congealed mince. The metromedia is dominated today by reports that Nicola offered Ed a coalition and got her proposal spurned, like the ugly sister begging the handsome prince to marry her. But that's not what happened. I was watching. Many of you would also have been watching, or you saw it on the news later.

For starters Ed Miliband is no handsome prince, he barely qualifies as a frog. He's got the starey eyes off pat though. But far more importantly than Ed's amphibious qualities we saw the exchange for ourselves and there was no offer of any coalition. But still we're being told there was. So it's either that we're surrounded by morons with the comprehension skills of baboons with dementia, or the media is deliberately misreporting what happened - it's hard to decide which of those two scenarios is worse. Although, come to think of it, they're not mutually exclusive.

But then the traditional media holds up a mirror to the traditional politicians, and the politicians are morons who tell lies and who don't even have the good grace to look ashamed when they get caught out. They just delete their Tweets and wait for the next spin of the news cycle, rinse, repeat. James Frances Murphy BA Politics (failed) was at it again today, launching Labour's Scottish manifesto at an invitation only event in a secret location in the East End of Glasgow which no East Enders had been invited to. The little people's presence isn't required, Jim knows what working class Scots think because he goes to fitba matches and sits in the directors' box along with John Reid. Whatever happened to John Reid? The only man in the Labour party less popular than Jim, at least until May 8.

Today the Murph E Coyote is saying, "We can't have rewards for the few and insecurity for the many." And that Jim, right there, is precisely why the Labour vote in Scotland has collapsed. Being one of the few who gets rewarded and refuses to accept all responsibility for anything that goes wrong, the spinning pawed one would know a lot about that. Just how are those expenses claims and London private land-lording doing Jim, hmm? Being lectured on fairness and equality by Jim Murphy is like being lectured on ethical journalism by Andy Coulson.

Labour had 13 years of crushing majorities to prevent the few being rewarded while the many grew increasingly insecure. Instead we got zero hours contracts, bankers running riot, student fees, creeping privatisation, PFI, social mobility reduced and a widening chasm opened up between the richest and the rest of society - and Jim voted enthusiastically for all of it. Then during the referendum campaign last year the Labour party forgot about the Internationale and sang the God Save the Queen with the Tories while Jim responded to an egg like it was a suicide bomber with ebola. Now when Jim's political career is disappearing up his own backside more rapidly than Jim climbed up the backside of Tony Blair, he suddenly discovers he's a socialist. This is an announcement as believable as Katie Hopkins joining the Workers Revolutionary Party.

Labour's Scottish manifesto launch was dominated, not by the many flavours of invisible promissory jam which were being larded about like profit forecasts at a pyramid sellers' convention, but by dire warnings about the SNP. Labour is obsessed. They are so consumed with hatred and fear of the SNP that they are still trapped in a time warp in 1979.

For everyone under the age of 40, 1979 was when SNP MPs voted against Jim Callaghan's Labour government in a vote of confidence. This came after Labour had shafted Scotland in the infamous 1979 referendum on very limited home rule, but in Labourland this betrayal has been airbrushed out of history just like Wee Dougie Alexander's Tweets. In his memoirs, Callaghan himself laid the blame for his government's demise on a number of his own backbenchers. However in the mythology of the Labour party, which is incapable of accepting that it might have any blame for anything at all, it's all the fault of the SNP that in the subsequent General Election, millions of people voted Tory. It certainly wasn't the fault of the Labour party for being unelectable.

Being trapped in the 1970s explains a number of things about Jim. It explains his condescending Mad Man debating tactics when faced with a woman opponent for starters. It also explains his decision to wrap himself in tartan, as he's convinced himself that he's a member of the Bay City Rollers and will be able to keep up his career long shag a-lang with his expenses claims. Never mind Jim, once we've voted you out of office you can disappear from public view, and in your occasional appearances in Where are they now? articles in the Daily Record, illustrated with your trademark halo backlighting, you can boast that you're still big in Japan and are booked to appear in Fukushima, juggling eggs for a few yen.

Jim only gets away with it because he is rarely subjected to forensic examination, such is the deference the Labour party has traditionally enjoyed in Scotland from a media that doesn't bother to report accurately even those things we've all seen for ourselves. A media that misuses words. A media that doesn't take care with words is a media that chancers like Jim can use to deceive. Taking Labour in Scotland seriously is a crime against words.

We have a media which doesn't care about words, yet words are supposed to be the stock in trade of writers and reporters. It's like a builder who doesn't give a shit about the building materials they use. And then the house falls down trapping us in the rubble while the builder walks away. We need a new one, a solid one, a sturdy one, and with our words, we are building a new media all by ourselves, fighting tabloids with tablets. Because words are important, words are magic. Watch them make careerist chancers disappear.

## Schrodinger's Labour

*19 April 2015*

We're in that period before Christmas when the prezzies have already been wrapped up in an Ashcroft poll and put under the tree. Have we got that Murph E Coyote doll we asked for? The one that runs off the canyon edge keeping aloft on its own frantic spinning, only to fall and land with a resounding splat in a dustcloud of McTernans. The special edition Scottish Labour model, the one that comes with additional features, like extra hubris and a smug look that can be wiped off its face. It's one of those toys that are only fun when you smash them.

There's a Murph E Coyote shaped package under the tree, and when you shake it it's got that reassuring death rattle. It's certainly looking good, for those who want substantial more power for Scotland if not for James Francis Murphy BA Politics (failed). But is it really the prezzie we long for, or will we be disappointed and only get a pair of hand knitted Westminster featherbedders. The signs are good, but we won't know for sure until we open the prezzie on May 7. In the meantime we've got a Schrodinger's Murph - Labour in Scotland is quantum, neither alive nor dead but in both states simultaneously.

The living death of zombie Labour was illustrated in the obsessive knee jerking of Kezia Dugdale when interviewed on Sunday's BBC Politics show. She was asked about the manifesto that Labour launched on Friday. The Dugless one was asked by Gordon Brewer about the cuts that Labour has said they'll have to introduce. No matter how he phrased the question, no matter what he asked or how he asked it, her answer to every question about Labour policy was, "The SNP is really bad and have bad questions to answer badly. The bad bad SNP are really bad. The SNP want Full Fiscal Autonomy and that's bad. The bad SNP have bad questions to answer. The SNP want another referendum and that's bad. Did I say that the SNP are really badly bad and have to answer bad questions, because the SNP are really bad. That's how bad they are, really bad, SNP bad. And finally, because this is an important point, I'd just like to mention that the SNP are really bad. I have so answered your question Gordon." Badly.

Kezia and the Labour party are too dense to realise that answering criticisms of their party with attacks on another party is an implicit acceptance on the proposition. When the only answer to the question - "Just how rubbish is your party?" is "But the SNP are more rubbish." You are accepting that your own party is rubbish and expecting people to listen to an attack originating from a party which tacitly acknowledges that it's rubbish. But then we already know that Labour is rubbish. That's why they're doing so poorly in the polls.

A woman who couldn't answer demanded that others answer so no one would notice she had no answers of her own. But we did notice, we do notice. We notice how bad Labour is. They don't stand for anything except keeping their careers, and hating the SNP. And they only hate the SNP because the SNP threatens their careers. It's not even a principled hatred.

In a desperate attempt to gain some purchase, Labour churns out policies from John McTernan's ACME catalog of spin, but it makes no difference. The reason is that Labour doesn't have a policy problem. It has a trust problem. It doesn't matter what policies you have if no one believes a word you say. And that lack of trust isn't down to the Murphoid one, although having a man who is a serial political cross dresser in charge really isn't helping Labour's bid for believability any.

It doesn't matter how many easy rides Jim gets in the media, no one will trust Labour until the party reforms itself. Labour has already been given numerous chances to reform itself, 2007, 2011, 2014 - and Labour's "reform" was to give us Jim Murphy. Jim Murphy is the Stars in their Political Eyes addict who wowed the metrocommentariat with his impressions. Today Matthew, Jim has painted his face blue and is wearing a Scotland shirt, next week he's donned a frock and is channelling Rosa Luxemburg. The week after that he'll be manning the barricades in the Paris Commune with a pile of Irn Bru crates. The week before the election he'll be camped out in a battery farm in the hope that someone throws an egg at him. But when you remove the hastily applied make up and the costumes, underneath Jim is still the Blairite chancer that he's always been. I know that, you know that, the dug knows that, we all know that.

It's so bad for Labour that the Sunday Herald has reported that Jim Murphy has sought legal advice on whether he can remain as leader of the tattered remnants of Labour in Scotland if he loses his own seat. The Smugurphy one denies that he's asked for legal advice on the issue. But then he would, wouldn't he.

There have been rumours of wriggle room in the clause in the constitution that says that a candidate for election to leadership must be an elected politician, but the rules are silent on what happens if a successful candidate loses their seat afterwards. In Jim's world it would be perfectly acceptable for a totally discredited leader to retain his position, but then he was totally discredited before he was elected, so to be fair there would be no real change there.

We are living in historic times. The death of the Labour party is being foretold in the signs and portents of polls and Kezias. Labour isn't spinning, it's a death spiral.

We can't take anything for granted. The polls are stupendously good for those who want to break the back of the old ways of doing things in Scotland, the secret deals and handshakes, the cosy agreements, the old boys' network, the careerists with a cushy seat for life. The polls are gobsmackingly good, unbelievably good, but the only vote that counts is the one on May 7.

Let's keep working. Let's open Schrodinger's box and find Labour's cat has expired. Let's see the cartoon until the end, and watch the coyote run off the cliff and fall to its doom in the dust. Labour in Scotland May 7 2015, that's all folks!

**Dear Martin**

*20 April 2015*

Dear Martin, thank you very much for your lovely letter which was sent out in a mail shot from the Labour party. Oh look, I said to myself, a letter from that guy who plays the hobbit in the movies and it's addressed to me personally. But sadly the only wizardry on display was the magic of mail merge, and that wasn't quite enough to convince me that you had actually sat down and directed yourself personally to my concerns. George Osborne might do a convincing impression of Sauron, but this isn't Middle Earth and Ed Miliband sure as hell isn't Gandalf. Middle Earth is a fantasy invented by a middle class guy from Oxford University, just like the claim of the modern Labour party to be a party of the left, come to think of it.

Thank you for assuming that I'm too thick to cope with the complexities of modern politics and require everything to be reduced to a binary opposition between Labour and the Tories. It's that kind of patronising attitude that has caused Labour to lose Scotland. You are offering a fantasy Martin, a story for children like dragons and orcs. In the real world, the one we actually live in as opposed to the fantasy one where Labour lives, we have other choices, and we can make our own minds up about what our choices are. There are other ways to resist the

Tories. Labour thinks it can resist the Tories by aping them, by turning itself into little monkeys who perform tricks for the Conservative press and offer working class people the occasional peanut. That's not resistance, and even a hobbit should realise that.

Despite what you say I'm not confused by different parties claiming different things, I can weigh up multiple options. And I can see that the simplistic choice you offer on behalf of the Labour party is a false one. But then you don't need to be a mental giant to resist the dubious charms of Jim Murphy. You don't need to be an Oxford don to see through Magrit Curran's lies. You don't need the wisdom of Gandalf to be unconvinced by Ed.

Labour can claim what they like, and even if they were offering a winning lottery ticket for every voter, a free foreign holiday and a guaranteed shag with someone who is actually attractive and who doesn't look like your average politician, I won't believe them if I don't trust them. And that's your problem right there, Martin. I don't trust the Labour party as far as I could throw it. And I could throw it as far as missile strike in Baghdad. I could throw Labour as far as an ATOS assessment. I could throw Labour as far as Ed Balls and his promise not to undo any of George Osborne's cuts. Labour has been promising invisible jam at every election I can remember, yet as soon as they get into power they morph into Murphy.

The choice I want to make is to prevent Labour from behaving like it has always done, to make Labour behave like a Labour party should. Voting Labour in Scotland doesn't offer me that choice, all voting Labour offers is a return to being side-lined, marginalised, ignored and patronised. I choose to hold Labour to account. I choose another way, a Scottish way.

The Labour party started in Scotland you say. And that would be true. And values of community, compassion and fairness still hold true you say. And that would be true as well, only they've got little or nothing to with the Labour party in Scotland. Labour sold those values down a PFI river decades ago, then contracted them out to ATOS for a profit. Because Martin, all those cruel and horrible things that the Tories pursue with gusto, Labour wants to keep them - the creeping privatisations, the disability assessments, the benefits caps, the demonisation of the poor, the dispossessed, the migrants, the worship of weapons of mass destruction. In Middle Earth Labour would be on the side of the orcs. Look at Jim Murphy and you can see they already are.

The Labour party was born in Scotland, and it will die in Scotland too. There's a poetic circularity to that if nothing else. Labour moved away from the communities that gave it root, and migrated to the City of London. Seduced by the precious ring of capital that promised absolute power, Labour deprived itself of its roots. So Labour shrivelled and died, cut off from the communities that gave it life and meaning and purpose. There is no point or purpose to the Labour party any more. They stand for nothing but power for power's sake, the party of careerists who don't know the difference between principles and press releases.

But those values of community, compassion, and fairness that you speak of Martin, they do still hold true, and unlike Labour they are alive and strong and breathing in the communities that gave birth to the Labour party. Like most in Scotland I hold them dear. It's just that they are no longer to be found in the Labour party. Us hobbits, us wee folk with our hairy Caledonian legs, we've created another party where we can express those values.

Today Martin, this Monday April 20, another party presented its manifesto to the electorate in Scotland. It is a manifesto that Labour would once have been proud to present. It promises social justice, and fairness and compassion and community. It promises to resist weapons of mass destruction, to fight for the disabled, to include the excluded, to bring tolerance and sense to the media's racist hysteria about immigration. It's a manifesto that promises to do all the things that Labour used to offer but never followed through on. Those things that Labour no longer even offers. It's a manifesto for Scotland, not a manifesto for the Tory press.

And unlike Labour's litany of lies and broken promises and shattered dreams - I can actually believe it. It's a manifesto that comes from a party that promises to lock out the Tories and to keep Labour on track. It's a party that really is a mass movement, born in Scotland's communities, unlike Labour's hollowed out shell, focus grouped to death. It's a party that can make sure that Labour has a spine, because Labour needs a moral conscience. When the Labour leadership are left to their own devices they find their moral conscience in Daily

Mail editorials, and then they hope to convince us with children's tales of orcs and hobbits presented by starry eyed stars. But we have our feet on the Scottish ground.

I vote for moral conscience, I vote for hope, I vote for compassion and care. And that Martin, is why I'm voting SNP.

## Being Scottish on Purpose

*21 April 2015*

John Major's really upset. No really. He's pure dead raging. There's going to be mayhem in May. The last Tory PM before this one gave a speech today, and people all over the country said, "Who? Oh, right, the grey puppet guy from Spitting Image. Is he still alive then?"

Some people in the hand-picked audience of spittle flecked Tory pensioners didn't fall asleep, that's how raging John was. He's raging at you, dear reader. You're mental. You're reckless and not in a Tory defector to UKIP sort of a way. Oh no, you are a clear and present danger to national security that's going to require the combined efforts of Johnny English, James Bond (but not the Sean Connery one), that guy from the Kingsmen movie who's dead posh, and a ninja columnist on the Telegraph to sort you out. Mind you, Alan Cochrane would put you off your dinner if he appeared in a zentai suit, although to be honest he does that anyway. Where's yer Alicsammin downfall now then Alan eh? Tee hee.

Anyway, having tried and failed to purge my mind of the image of Alan Cochrane in stretchy lycra, John has returned from the silence of the shires to slap you down because you are, and I hesitate to say this, of a Scottish persuasion. You are a monster. And you look like you're going to be deliberately Scottish at the General Election - you're even doing it on purpose. That's as much of a threat to all that is good and true and Great British family values as being gay was in the 1970s. It's unadulterated evil, and it's jolly well not on. You'd be marching in lycra next, if it wasn't for the fact that you're in need of therapy after thinking about Alan Cochrane. Although as everyone who doesn't work for the Telegraph knows, he's the one in need of therapy.

But it's OK. John has Scottish friends. He has friends like Michael Forsyth and the beardy guy in the properly unionist lycra suit who have their finger on the pulse of Scotland. They're completely representative of Scottish opinion and have told him that it's just fine to deprive Scotland of its democratic rights. "You can insult Scottish people John. Tell them it's OK, you have Scottish friends."

Scotland would only use democracy to keep Tories out of power, and that just isn't on at all. That's not what we're Better Together for, Scotland is supposed to be that small bit at the top of the BBC weather map where few seats change hands at Westminster Elections. Yet now, just look what's happened, Scottish people who aren't friends of John are insisting on making things interesting. John doesn't like it when things are interesting.

John knew this was going to happen. He warned us back in the 1990s that this devolution business was only going to end in tears. Tears for him and his Westminster pals that is. But oh no, some people decided that they had to let those Scottish people have a bit of democracy and now look what's happened. He's not naming any names but he's pointing his finger at the Labour party. It's their fault. It's not the fault of the Tories for ignoring the democratic aspirations of Scotland for a decade and a half. Oh no. That's just something Scotland has to suck up, being a part of this fine union.

John is shocked and appalled at the recent turn of events. You can tell he's angry, because he audibly harrumphed. He may even be forced to tap his fingers on his podium and tell us about his torrid nights with Edwina. You'll be sorry then, Scottish people.

Now Scottish people want more of it, democracy that is, not the Labour party or the Tories, and certainly not Edwina Curry. John has got used to Scotland not wanting the Tories but is alarmed because the Scots don't want the Labour party either. Because that means something truly awful, even more awful than Alan Cochrane - it means that Scottish people are insisting that they ought to have a say in how the UK is run. The glittery stardust of a thousand love-bombs is choking Westminster to death.

"But you said ..." chorus Scottish people, pointing to a Better Together leaflet that said how much the UK loves us, needs us, and values our contribution to British national life. We're only doing what they told us they wanted. We're injecting a dose of Scottish reality into the corridors of Westminster.

It's just not on you know. This is not what Better Together was all about. Better Together was supposed to mean that Scotland was better for being ruled by Westminster, not that Westminster could be better for having Scotland tell it how to do things. Yet here we are, just over two weeks away from a General Election, and the most interesting thing that's happening is John Major having a bit of a strop. Now if that's not rubbish politics I don't know what is.

John's come back from the political grave to give some soapbox gravitas to his successors, the modern Tory exponents of rubbish politics. He's been joined by the undead Michael Forsyth back from the political grave. Michael Forsyth chose politics as his career, he climbed to the top of the greasy pole of sycophants and became Thatcher's man in Scotland, and he led the Scottish Tories to a total rout in 1997, losing every single seat the party possessed. It's the only political achievement he's ever managed. Michael is the failure's failure, although he may be about to be surpassed by Jim Murphy who climbed to the top of an Irn Bru crate and destroyed the Labour party.

But the Tory warnings aren't about Scotland at all really. They're about shoring up the Tory vote in Englandshire and about delegitimising Scotland's votes. When Scotland returns a large body of MPs who are deemed to be beyond the pale by a slavering media, then the Tories hope that they can cling onto power on the back of English votes alone. They screech that the SNP want to drive a wedge between Scotland and England while they take a sledge hammer to the foundations of the United Kingdom. With every editorial, every spittle flecked denunciation, they destroy what they claim to hold dear.

They told us they loved us, they told us they wanted us. Well we're only giving them what they asked for, we're being Scottish on purpose, we're playing by their rules and kicking their arses in the process. A wise man once said that the secret of true wisdom was still to want what you longed for after you'd got it. There's not much wisdom in Westminster. The union is done for, and it's not Scotland that broke it.

## Explaining the Funny

*23 April 2015*

When you have to explain a joke, the funny dies. Which makes this blog post an exposition of death. Yesterday a wee joke made by Alicsammin a week or so back was examined from every possible angle. Inside, outside, upside down. It was held up to the window to see if it was transparently a joke and the massed ranks of the media metrocommentariat decided that it wasn't. Can you see through that with your London blinkers on? Oh no, this is a serious and deadly intervention in the general election campaign, they chorused. Because the rest of the national campaign has been, let's face it, pretty shite and they needed something - anything - to generate a bit of controversy and help spark some life into the Tories' ailing bid for re-election.

Monstering Scottish people is always good for that, since you can safely be racist about Scots seeing as how they've not immigrated anywhere. Except for Michael Gove and Liam Fox, but they don't count because they are *Toriores Tories ipsis*. However there's a big threat to Westminster from a large bloc of SNP MPs who are threatening to migrate into the corridors of power and be deliberately Scottish in lobbies and committees. That can't be allowed to happen. Scotland might think having

Westminster held to ransom by a squad of angry Scottish people is a bit of a laugh, but the Tory press can't see the joke. But then you never can see the joke when the joke is on you. It's like Davie Cameron trying to read the "kick me" sign in tartan paint that's been pinned to the back of his jaicket.

But treating a joke as not a joke provided a media with a chance to monster Alicsammin, who's the monsterers' monster of choice. So even though it was as transparently a joke as Boris Johnson's haircut or anything that Magrit Curran ever says or does, although unlike them it was meant to be funny on purpose, it was to be taken seriously. A Tory election campaign depends upon scaring the shiters out of UKIP leaning voters in the leafy shires with the invention of Scottish Nationalists who will them pay for all the drinks, the peanuts, and then afterwards making them pay for an immigrant kebab.

So the joke was picked apart, dissected and stuffed into the Large Hadron Collider then wheeched around at the speed of light and smashed at the quantum level. It was helpfully deconstructed by some Unionists affecting a feminist perspective who pondered its implications for an undermined Nicola. Musings were mused by the unamused about whether a throwaway line hid a deeper truth, and the consensus was that of course it did, because it came from Alicsammin. Alicsammin is Gaelic for Beelzebub. The deeper truth is that Alicsammin is evil, it always is. Alicsammin wants to eat babies and make the English pay for the tomato sauce.

The funny, of which there was not a large quantity to begin with, was extracted and freeze dried then pinned down on a board like a dead butterfly bleached of all colour. And when you suck out the colour from a butterfly you're left with a moth eaten Daily Mail headline. Alicsammin's going to write the Labour budget, screamed the Tory press. Run for those wee elevations that pass for hills!

This was all so some humourless twunks could distract attention from an even less funny joke made by Davie Cameron earlier in the day, when he likened Alicsammin to a pick pocket. Oh how we chortled. And guess which one of these jokes BBC Scotland decided to run with? Repeatedly.

This is a peculiar election campaign. With most of the focus on Scotland, the UK media and political parties seems to have given up any real interest in the proceedings, like a surly teenager who's annoyed not to be the centre of attention at someone else's birthday party. And this time it's a Scottish party.

We've got two weeks to go until the vote, and there are no signs that the advance of the SNP is about to be halted. Just about everything has been rolled out in the tried and trusted untrustworthiness of Project Fear Mark 2. The Tories gave up on Scotland years ago, meanwhile Labour's leadership - the real leadership not the branch office management - seem to have joined them and have abandoned the hapless Murph E Coyote to his inevitable plunge off the canyon edge. Now it's all about shoring up their votes in England and Wales, and trying to grab as many votes as they can back from the grasping and flailing paws of UKIP.

In Scotland the SNP juggernaut rolls on, threatening to crush all before it. Labour seems to have given up in many seats, concentrating its meagre resources in mail shots delivered by the Royal Mail because Labour doesn't have activists on the ground. Labour MPs who previously barely knew where their constituencies were have been seeing going round the doors, cutting lonely and forlorn figures on the doorstep, standing on the threshold of their party's extinction. They're paying the price for taking us for granted, no wonder they can't see the joke.

Instead of giving Scotland what Scotland has told the Unionist parties repeatedly what it wants, Labour and the Tories give us allegations of bullying. It's what bullies do when they're losing. Scottish people are being nasty to the nasty bullies, and that's just nasty. Only Labour and the Tories are allowed to be nasty. They're licenced to be nasty, they're professionally nasty. Freelance nastiness is beyond the pale, mockery is worse than an ATOS assessment, a cutting remark is worse than blowing up a wedding party in Afghanistan.

The hysterical hyperbole of the Unionist press is a joke, but it's not funny on purpose. It's met with derision and disparagement. And this is how the Union ends, in Scottish laughter and jeering, in satire and scorn. We're scoffing and mocking our way to a country where our concerns can be taken seriously. Scotland isn't just going to write a Labour budget, we're going to write the terms of Union too. The joke is on Westminster.

## The Rationality of Rage

*24 April 2015*

There's an article in today's Guardian in which assorted Labour party figures bewail the supposedly irrational rage that their candidates encounter on the doorstep in Scotland. The public is so angry that punters refuse even to take Labour's literature, regarding it as radioactive waste, poisonous and contaminating. See thae voters, they're mad so they are. What have Labour ever done to deserve this? It makes no sense to the Guardian columnists and the party hierarchy. It's not the party which is wrong, it's the people. It's not Labour which has gone astray, it's Scotland.

The anger and contempt with which Labour is met is everyone's fault but Labour's - Wee Dougie Alexander thinks it's down to a European-wide phenomenon of anti-government feeling exacerbated by the banking crisis which in Scotland, as elsewhere in Europe, has found expression in a populist nationalism. And at that point we all stop listening.

It's got fuck all to do with that Dougie. It's because we know that Scotland isn't important enough to the Labour party for you to prioritise what Scottish voters want. It's got everything to do with voters in Scotland being sick fed up of a Labour party which has taken us for granted for generations while it ignores our wishes and sooks up to Tory voters in Middle England in an attempt to get into power. It's got everything to do with Labour turning itself into a vehicle for government which has no clue what to do once it gets into power except to pander to the right wing press and the financial services industry of the City of London. You had your 13 years of crushing Labour majorities under Blair and Brown Dougie. And you blew it.

Dougie, the root cause for Scotland's rage against Labour lies squarely with the Labour party. It lies with you Dougie, and with the rest of the sorry misbegotten bunch of placepersons, triangulators, schemers, pseudo-intellectuals, despair mongerers and party balloons who sit for Labour in Scotland. Dougie's rationale is "big boys done it and ran away" dressed up in the cant of pseudo-sophisticated sophistry.

Rage is a rational response to politicians who don't know the difference between truth and play dough. Rage is right when faced with an MP who thinks turning up for a photo shoot means they can take credit for a community campaign. Rage is the responsible response to those who have taken a party born in the struggle for social justice and turned it into a party of managing working class aspirations on behalf of the bosses. Rage is reasonable when confronted with a political class which is incapable of a straight answer to the simplest of questions. Jim Murphy couldn't even answer the question "do you want sugar with your tea" without uttering the words, "Look, I hope you don't mind."

I do mind Jim. I mind that you can't say whether you intend to resign your seat in East Renfrew in order to stand for Holyrood. I mind that you are unable to tell us exactly what cuts your party is planning. I mind that you manipulate facts to suit your arguments, I mind that you patronise, I mind that you interrupt, I mind that you went to work on an egg. I mind that you lie about socialism. I mind that you have no political principles beyond saving your sorry career. I mind that you're really using mind in the Scots sense and hoping we can't remember your expenses claims, your cheerleading for wars, your obsession with phallus shaped missiles. But we do fucking mind, as you will be reminded. And we're going to remind Labour that rage is righteous.

Rage is what happens when a people feel betrayed. It's the justified anger of the thrice scorned, the correct reply to the wrong question, it's the four minute warning to a party that's turned its back on the communities that gave it birth. And even now, despite the howling klaxons, Labour still can't hear, still doesn't want to listen.

The sirens shriek the death of Labour, and here we bloody go again with Gordie Broon being dragged out to vow things. Gordon Brown is getting increasingly like one of those elderly incontinent yappy wee dugs drooling in its toothless jaws as it tries to gain some purchase on your leg so it can shaft you - vowvowvowvow. He's promising all sorts of sweeties if only we vote Labour. That's the Gordie who was going to personally supervise the vow he swore before the referendum in front of the mass rank of an invited audience of a Labour supporter, some reporters from friendly newspapers and a BBC

66

camera. That one didn't end well, but here he is intervening for the first time again - only this time it's just rank.

This intervention is the last throw of the dice of a party that's gone beyond desperate. They're dragging out the pensionscarer again to speak in a closed locked room to a rank of reporters replacing a rally. A retiring MP with no power to do anything except remind us how useless he was the last time he made a vow.

This time Gordie is promising £5000 for every foodbank in Scotland. Is he going to personally ensure that promise is kept too? He's not promising to abolish food banks, he's not promising an end to the punitive benefits regime and the demonisation of the poor and needy. He's not promising to listen and learn. He's sure as hell not vowing that Labour will change. In Labour's eyes it doesn't need to change, it's us who need to change. Labour wants us to change back into the tame controlled flock of the unthinking that bends over to act as a footstool for its political ambitions.

So all we are left with is rage. Our rage will be the death of Labour in Scotland. Watch us, watch us kill off Labour with the laughter of the justified and the scorn of those who've been ignored too long. We've already pushed the party out of our hearts, now we stand on the edge of Labour's precipice, waiting for the satisfying splat of crushed careers. Our rage is rational. Our rage is reasonable. Our rage is cool, calm, and considered. And such rage, directed, will change the world.

## The Obituaries from Elderslie

*25 April 2015*

So there's this politician who is constantly intervening for the first time in the election campaign. Yes, it's Gordie Broon again, only this time he's not saving the wuld or even the banks, he's not even saving the Union. The wuld, in case you were wondering, is the world where Gordie lives. It doesn't seem to be planet Earth. It's the wuld where Gordie is a superhero, the same wuld where the Daily Record is published. It's the wuld where people believe in Gordie's estimation of himself.

This time Gordie's intervening in the campaign in order to save Wee Dougie Alexander's career. It's a bit of a come down, but then Gordie's stock has been in decline for a while. He intervenes in election campaign for the first time to give Labour a quick thrill, and then goes away for a day or so before coming back to intervene for the first time again. Gordie is in and out more frequently than a vibrator on a pogo stick. Only this time the batteries are dead.

Gordie's services are required by the wee skanktimonious one as his parliamentary career is about to be shafted by a lassie who was two when Dougie was first elected as an MP in 1997. This is happening despite

Wee Dougie being a giant on Labour's stage, at least when he can wrest the Irn Bru crates off Jim. Dougie has designs on the post of foreign secretary, but he's discovered that he's alien to most of his own constituents. So in an effort to appear at least vaguely human, he's called for help from Gordie, the only man in Labour who's more of a space cadet than Dougie or Jim Murphy.

Gordie's spaceship landed in Elderslie, where Gordatron Prime made an important and headline grabbing intervention in the election campaign which consisted, as it always does, of delivering a speech in front of a tiny invited audience of party loyalists, some telly cameras, and a few reporters. The speech has of course already been released to trusted journalists, who can then conveniently report what he will say, and then again what he actually said. This gives Gordie two bites of the intervention cherry, which is as close to a double orgasm as Labour's ever likely to get. And both of them would be faked.

Gordie is retired, but not retiring, and holds no position within the party he speaks to, or rather at. Gordie only does monologues, he doesn't answer questions - certainly not about that vow - and he won't ever appear in front of the unvetted punters on whose behalf he claims to speak. Because the punters might beg to disagree. Gordie doesn't like it when people disagree, because he'd have to go off script. Spontaneity is not covered by the pre-released press release, and Gordie might call someone a bigot.

This time the massed rank of the Labour supporter was treated to a disquistion on the evil SNP. Which was pretty much the same as the last speech Gordie made, and the one before that, and the one before that. Anyway, this time Gordie wanted us to know that the SNP was evil because they might put having another referendum in their manifesto in a different election entirely to the one we're having, and then people in Scotland might vote for it. And this would be a very bad thing. And wrong. And not a good thing. It would be eh, democracy, and we can't be having that. Gordie knows what's good for us. Don't think for yourself, it only leads to SNPness.

Instead of deciding things for ourselves, Scottish voters would be much better off listening to Gordie. He's vowing that if we vote for the Labour party then they'll guarantee to write a letter inviting companies to a conference to talk about maybe taking on a few unemployed people on work placements instead of sanctioning their benefits. However there will be tea and biscuits, at the conference that is, not for the folk who might have their benefits sanctioned, who will be expected to bring their own pieces. Jam won't be provided. Gordie isn't guaranteeing that Labour will put an end to benefits sanctions, but Gordie did give a guarantee that he will ensure that the letters are stamped and taken to the post box, and that's a vow. A second class vow, but then so was the last one.

Gordie also promised to abolish exploitative zero hours contracts, which is exactly what Labour was promising in 1997, when Gordie was going to be chancellor and might have been able to do something about zero hours contracts. So we're only 18 years late, but then he was too busy putting an end to boom and bust before having to save the wuld from going bust. However now that the wuld has been saved, and most of us are bust, he's going to personally guarantee that Jim Murphy will write a letter inviting businesses to another conference where they can discuss what "exploitative" means in relation to zero hours contracts. Then they kick the whole thing into the long grass just like they did in 1997.

Mainly however, Gordie wanted us to know that only by voting Labour can we be safe from the Tories. Except of course those Tories that the Labour party is going to invite into government as advisors, like Michael Heseltine. So presumably Labour's only going to save us from exploitative Tories, and not those deemed to be non-exploitative by Ed Balls and Chuka Umunna. If Labour does manage to secure a majority, their government is already shaping up to be as Laboury as the Blair and Broon combo, and we all know how socialist that one turned out to be.

This charade gets repeated with turgid regularity in the pages of the Scottish press and on the screens of Scottish broadcasters. It's the same with Jim Murphy BA Politics (failed) and his mass outdoor rallies of a wee group of what look like Labour studenty types. It's always the same wee group waving the same wee cardboard slogans. The camera is kept in close, no long shots to show us the truth of the lack of massness of the rally.

Con-tricks and make believe are Labour's stock in trade. They only get away with it because the media colludes and is an active participant in the charade. But no one believes either of them anymore. The lies and deceit hung in the air in the stale atmosphere of a closed meeting, locked away behind closed doors. Locked away like a coffin. The media reports are Labour's obituary from Elderslie.

Today in Glasgow there were two mass rallies that really were mass rallies, the people of Scotland are building a new political reality, and building a new media. We have no need of Gordie and his stale promises. Life moves on in the streets, and Labour's left behind. We won't look back. The future is already here.

## The Hope of the Wow

*27 April 2015*

Who needs the Vow when we've got wow? We've not only got wow, we've got utter gorgeousness. Eat yer heart out George Galloway. A couple of opinion polls were published on Monday, one a proper actual opinion poll of voters in Scotland with a representative sample and everything. The other was possibly somewhat less scientific, being an online poll of horny Edinburgh gay guys looking for a shag on Grindr.

This is of course tautological, as being on Grindr means that you are by definition a horny gay guy looking for a shag. And these days it's also getting tautological to state that opinion polls of Scottish voting intentions show that Labour has been totally screwed, nailed to the wall, whammed, bammed and no thank you jam. The poll discovered that 62% of horny gay guys in Edinburgh plan to vote SNP. Proof, as if any proof was needed, that voting SNP means you get sexy, and that the SNP has got the gay vote pretty much sewn up in a glamorous clutch bag.

Grindr, for those of you of a shy and retiring heterosexual disposition, is an app for gay men who are looking for a random shag. It doesn't tend to be used by men who are looking to settle down and get a Labrador together. Most guys who use Grindr claim to have unfeasibly large wullies, because profiles on Grindr are about as accurate as Labour party manifesto promises and likewise invariably end in disappointment.

The guy who carried out the poll did a similar poll just before the independence referendum, and got a result which was pretty much spot on in terms of the actual vote. Which only goes to show that horny gay guys are more representative of the population at large than UKIP would care to admit.

The proper poll, carried out for TNS, showed that the SNP currently has the support of 54% of Scotland's voters. On these figures, and given a uniform national swing, Labour will be left with just one seat in Scotland. Which would mean that Wee Wullie Bain would be Secretary of State for Scotland in a Miliband government because he'd be the only Labour MP left.

Unfortunately for Wee Wullie, the only certain thing about a universal national swing is that it's entirely mythical. Swings are never uniform, and the swing to the SNP looks like it's much stronger in the Glasgow area, where some figures suggest the SNP could hoover up 60% of the vote. So Wee Wullie would be out on his ear too. I recently spent some time with Anne McLaughlin, the SNP candidate in Glasgow East, interviewing her for an article for Newsnet Scotland - and it's fair to say that Wee Wullie doesn't look like he's got very many fans on Grindr. This is despite the fact that Labour really does have an unfeasibly large dick in the shape of Jim Murphy.

Jim is now bereft of ideas. He's tried to bombard us with promises of jam. Whatever happened to the Vow Plus? Gordie gets trotted out with alarming regularity to vow things that get quietly forgotten about a few days later when they've been slapped down by the Labour leadership in London.

Over the weekend the promise to give a wee bit of jam - quite literally - to food banks in Scotland evaporated like spilt milk in the sunshine, leaving nothing behind but a stain and a bad smell. And the promise to abolish "exploitative" zero hours contracts collapsed in the contradiction of a Labour council which employs 2000 workers on zero hours contracts. So they're not exploitative when Labour uses them. Labour is the party of do as I say not do as I do. They are out of ideas, out of inspiration, out of hope. Labour is the no-trick pony. They're just pony.

But it doesn't matter anymore when no one trusts a word you say, and that's Jim's real problem, and because of that fact he's staring an extinction level event in the face. There's an asteroid on a collision course with the Labour party in Scotland, and the only defence Jim has got left is a tattered umbrella saying SNP bad. The dinosaur complains about the shortcomings of mammals as the fireball lights up the sky.

Jim was at it again today, standing beside Ed Balls and repeating SNP bad to a small audience of Labour activists and press representatives. And this is another example of tautology because Labour never has any other kind of audience these days. If Jim Murphy or Gordie Broon ever did give a speech to an audience of ordinary non-party affiliated Scottish people that really would be news. But that's as likely to happen as a horny gay guy on Grindr being honest about the size of his wullie.

A part of me weeps that it has come to this. Labour is the junkie child, a product of Scottish communities. But Labour is a part of the family who has gone bad. The only recourse remaining is to kick the badjin out and let it fend for itself without sooking off expenses accounts, because otherwise it just keeps hurting us, it keeps sticking in the knife and turning it. And Labour does that because it takes us for granted like it always has done. Even now, on the edge of extinction it can't believe that it won't be forgiven and all its sins forgotten. It's not like we've not given it fair warning. It's not like we've not given it chances, but Labour keeps nicking the cash from our purses and the faith from our hearts. It's beyond redemption.

Last year the independence referendum showed voters in Scotland that we can still hope of things getting better. We can still hope that our voices will be heard and our opinions count. That is what this election is about for Scotland, hope. We've learned how to hope and we're not going to squander it on Labour's Grindr profile. Hope is what is driving the opinion polls, but Project Fear is determined to put us back in our shortbread tin. Jim had pinned all his hopes on a late swing, and there is a late swing, it's just not in the direction Jim was hoping for.

This time it isn't going to work - there is an army of us spreading the message that hope still lives. We need to keep up the pressure, but we're in for a rocky ride over the next few days. Let's keep working, let's keep hope alive. We've got the hope of the wow.

## Whatever Happened to Baby Jim?

*28 April 2015*

Labour is like a gambling addict, convinced that the next throw of the dice will bring about a turn in its fortunes. They believe this even though they've thrown the dice out of the window and into the path of the oncoming Caledonian express that's about to flatten them.

Following a series of brutal opinion polls which suggest that Labour is facing extinction in Scotland, Jim Murphy BA Politics (failed) and his fellow subscribers to the John McTernan ACME catalogue of fears, smears and Toryesque policies have decided to embark on a radically new strategy. And that new course of direction, that thing that they've never tried before, that stroke of genius - that would be obsessively slagging off the SNP and screaming from the rooftops that they're really really bad. And probably Nazis, and Communists, and definitely obsessed with Mel Gibson movies, and totally obsessed with the referendum - the SNP that is, not the Labour party.

The Labour party aren't obsessed at all, like Bette Davis in Whatever Happened to Baby Jim, they're still stars and will be serving up a cooked rat and blaming it on the SNP just before they attempt to push Scotland down a flight of stairs to the accompaniment of a 1920s show tune. That's perfectly sane and rational.

No really, slagging off the SNP is a new thing, well according to the Labour party, and they wouldn't lie would they. Although if Jim Murphy believes that anyone will be convinced that this is a new thing or that Labour wouldn't lie then somewhere there must be a box of frogs which is really relieved to discover that it is not after all the maddest thing in the universe. For the rest of us Labour's demise is ribbitting.

Now that Jim's scheme to court Yes voters by donning a fitba shirt, making a song and dance about milking English taxpayers, and legalising drink fuelled sectarianism has proven as attractive as being stalked by an identity thief who's got millions in a Nigerian bank account he needs your help to unblock, Labour has moved on to Plan Con - begging Tory voters for help. Although to be fair, all of Jim's plans have been a con. It's just that they've been pathetically transparent, and so is his latest.

The SNP is very very bad, according to Jim, because they're going to press ahead with a second referendum. That would be the second independence referendum that the SNP isn't asking for, but because it wasn't specifically ruled out in the SNP manifesto, Labour insists that the SNP are going to press ahead with one anyway. There are of course lots of things that were not specifically ruled out in the SNP manifesto which are very likely to happen after the election - for example grief therapy and counselling for the Labour party in Scotland, or an appointment at the job centre for Blairites who'll discover why sanctions aren't such a good thing after all - but a second referendum isn't one of them. Jim is hoping that by fighting a referendum campaign that isn't actually happening he can scare up a few Tories to vote for him, and save his arse in East Renfrewshire - which is one of the few seats where there are enough Tories to make a difference. It is, after all, all about Jim, and it always has been.

Jim made this pronouncement while campaigning in the East End of Glasgow along with Magrit Curran, and Caroline Flint who had been invited along to give a bit of Labour leadership gravitas to Jim's Bette Davis impression. Jim and Magrit were filmed by some telly cameras standing beside a building site and a very big hole. Yet again Labour had organised a campaigning event in Glasgow without inviting any actual Glaswegians, because some of the kinder ones might have yelled at Jim and Magrit to stop digging, while others would have shown them how to operate the JCB.

Working class Glaswegians don't tend to be Tory voters, and so aren't really Jim's target audience. So not really a campaigning event then, it was an astroturf event, only without any turf, astro or otherwise. There was no one there except Jim, Magrit, Caroline and a couple of press people. Jim must be longing for the days when the punters gave enough of a shit to turn up just so they could shout back at him.

However the Labour party in Scotland's attempts to stop itself from drowning with the aid of inflatable Tory floaters are being scuppered by the tidal waves generated of the Labour party leadership as it flails about in some deep water of its own. That would be the real Labour party leadership, not Jim's branch managerial variety. Ed Miliband has - for the second time in the past few weeks - insisted that he would block a second independence referendum. This may help him in his attempts to woo voters in England, but in Scotland all it does is to tell voters who haven't yet made up their minds that they can vote SNP safe in the knowledge that by doing so they're not voting for another referendum.

Meanwhile, with the help of the Daily Mail - Kezia Dugdale's favourite go-to publication for photos of her looking miserable and sad - the Tories are stoking the fires of English nationalism, according to Labour and the Lib Dems. It doesn't seem to have occurred to them that they themselves were merrily stoking the fires of English nationalism during the independence referendum when they told Scots we were the recipients of English largesse and ought to be grateful. It's only bad when the Tories do it, because this might damage Labour and the Lib Dems.

Time is running out now. There are few spins left for Labour's one armed bandits. Unless something really dramatic happens between now and next Thursday, the game is a bogey for Labour. The compulsive gamblers will have dealt their last cards, and lost badly. It's a safe bet they'll still blame everyone else for their own misfortunes, and like Baby Jane they'll dance on the beach oblivious to the men in white coats coming to take them away for good.

## The Third Lanark of Politics

*29 April 2015*

Labour's plummeting poll statistics prove that it is actually possible for something to plunge more quickly than gravitational force and laws of physics would allow. But then Newton never thought to include public disgust and opprobrium in his calculations. The 45 are going to give Labour MPs their P45s, and there may be no Labour MPs left in Scotland by the end of next week. The word pandafication has entered the political lexicon.

According to a report in the Torygraph, senior Labour figures in Scotland are demanding that Jim Murphy BA Politics (failed) resigns as leader of Labour's branch office in Scotland after the election. Despite the portents of impending doom, it is rumoured that the Murph E. Coyote intends to cling on to the cliff edge of leadership even if he's kicked off his seat by his constituents and the shell shocked band of Labour MSPs, cooncillors and ex-MPs hammer at his grasping paws with rolled up copies of the Labour party rule book.

The in-fighting in Labour has already broken out into the open, with reports of cooncillors refusing to support the re-election campaigns of their local Labour MP just in case their political death is contagious. So it's not just the punters who will be glad to see the back of certain Labour MPs. The walking dead of the Labour party in Scotland are already demanding a victim, they wanting a post mortem before the execution and Jim is going to be offered up for ritual sacrifice. We've not even had the vote yet and already the recriminations have started - which I suppose makes then precriminations.

I sat down with some doritos and sour cheese dip to watch Jim Murphy getting interviewed live by STV's Bernard Ponsonby. Well I say "live", but he was really a political corpse. There was plenty of sour cheese on display from Jim, but the dip was far more solid and substantial. Bernard asked Jim about the dire opinion polls and whether he took responsibility for Labour's impending demise. The rapidly greying Jim said it wasn't really about him as an individual - and across Scotland people were shouting at their tellies - "Yes it is Jim. Yes it is." Jim is still denying that he's in denial about the dire straits his party is in.

He's also denying he's going to make any cuts, he'll be making "savings". We all know that Labour's going to make cuts. Jim's problem is that no one in the Labour leadership has told him what they're going to be. He's going to pay for all the extra goodies he's promising with extra taxes, like a tax on banks which apparently is mostly going to be raised outside Scotland. Although during the indyref Jim was one of those who spent his time telling us that the banks were Scottish. Labour is as consistent on that one as they are on the safety of the NHS. The NHS was safe during the indyref, according to Labour, and it was only evil nationalist separatists who said it was under threat. But now Labour tells us that the NHS is under threat and only the people who didn't realise it was under threat can save it. It's all very confusing in Jim's mental universe. Perhaps that's the reason his eyebrows appear to be living separate lives.

Jim wants extra powers for the Scottish Parliament, because Jim's a patriot. He doesn't want the extra powers that the SNP want, because they're unpatriotic extra powers. Jim only wants patriotic powers. Like powers over benefits that Labour ruled out during the Smith Commission negotiations. Perhaps Labour only ruled them out then so that Jim could patriotically demand them now.

Bernard moves on to asking Jim about a letter he wrote to Tricia Marwick, the Presiding Officer of the Scottish Parliament. Jim had wanted Tricia to make a ruling that MSPs should be banned from having two jobs. But isn't that exactly what Jim is proposing for himself? Hmmm? Jim wants to be a full time MP and then stand for Holyrood next year and be a full time First Minister. So does the two jobs thing not apply to him? Jim says it won't apply to him, because - he doesn't add - it was of course just a means of getting a wee dig in a Alicsammin. Not having two jobs outside politics of course was what he really meant, he says in that soft creepy voice of his. Except that Alicsammin's two jobs were both in politics too. Jim hopes we don't notice that bit. But we do Jim. We do. And so do voters in East Renfrew.

Bernard asks him - So will you be a full time MP? Jim won't answer. Will you be a part time First Minister then?

Won't answer. Mind you it's not really relevant, because he won't have any job at all by the end of next week.

Finally there was the obligatory fitba reference, and Bernard asked Jim if the SNP were Real Madrid, which team would Labour be. Clearly the answer is Third Lanark, because they're extinct too. Anyway, the only thing we learned from that entire interview was that Bernard is a Celtic fan. Jim's still talking mince, still not answering questions, and still doing an impression of a sour cheese dip that's well past its sell by date.

Libby Brooks, the Guardian's Scottish correspondent whose main claim to fame is that she isn't Severin Carrell, called Jim's performance "quality". Which was accurate, as long as you prefixed it with "poor" or "pish". Or possibly she hadn't been paying any attention and was asking if there were any of the soft centred Quality Streets left.

The only thing you can be certain of with an interview with Jim Murphy is that he won't answer any of the questions, but then he spends all his time talking over the top of everyone else, so to be fair he probably doesn't know what the question is. The answer, we all know by now, isn't Jim Murphy.

## The Last Squawk

*1 May 2015*

Oh furgodssake. I was planning an evening putting my feet up, scoffing at the debates on the telly like a normal person, and then having an early night with a box set of Battlestar Galactica and a meringue, and Ed Miliband only goes and spoils it all by putting the final nail in Jim Murphy's coffin. So I have to write something, and there's me been resisting temptation all day.

So, deep in the rain forests of South America, linguists discovered a parrot that was the last speaker of a language whose human users had long since died out. All that's known of this language are a few words squawked by a parrot which has no idea what they mean. And that's also a fair description of socialism and the Labour party in Scotland. But parrots at least can have bright red plumage, there's nothing red left about Labour.

It hasn't been easy resisting the temptation to blog something. Labour is the satirical gift that keeps on giving. First off there was David Blunkett complaining that the biggest threat to democracy was that people in Scotland aren't listening to Labour any more, and not you know, that Labour should maybe be listening to Scottish people. In Blunkettworld it's the job of the electorate to listen to political parties. If he believes that then it explains a whole lot about Labour's behaviour when in office, and illustrates perfectly why Labour needs to be held to account by a big bloc of SNP MPs standing over them with a voting lobby baseball bat.

Then Jim Murphy had a car crash of an interview on Reporting Scotland with Sally Magnusson. In the normal scheme of things a Labour politician getting a rough ride on Reporting Scotland is like the princess complaining that there's a pea under her pile of mattresses. However Jim's been lying in Labour's pee for so long that even Reporting Scotland can no longer ignore the stench. Jim spent the entire interview not answering any of the questions Sally put to him, preferring instead to squawk about Davie Cameron rubbing his hands in glee at the prospect of Scotland voting for a party that hates him even more than Labour does. This may make sense in Jim's universe, but it doesn't in anyone else's. Sally didn't give him a cracker, and a few more undecided voters decided that they weren't going to vote for Jim's bonhomie of the bonfire, smugging while Labour burns.

So there was that, and then came the leader interviews on Question Time when Davie, Nick and Ed faced questions from punters. All of them were keen to let us know that they hold no truck with any deals with the SNP because the SNP are communist nazi feminist misogynists who want to break up this great country of ours.

Now there are some languages, some of which may be spoken by parrots in the Amazon, which have more than one word for "our". There's the our in the sense of "belonging you me, you, and others", and there's the our in the sense of "belonging to me and others but not you". UK politicians demonstrate a new sense of the word our in the phrase "this great country of ours", and that would be "belonging to the British establishment but not the Scottish people". Because they're all quite determined that Scottish voters will get no say in how it's governed.

Just when you thought that Labour in Scotland was already closer to an extinction event and deeper in the doo doo than a paralytic parrot with dysentery, Ed Miliband went and made it worse. No really, it was possible to do that and Ed did. Hell yeah. He tied the Murphmacaw up in a sack full of bricks and tossed him in the Union Canal. Then he jumped up and down on top of the sack to make sure that it sank to the bottom, getting himself half drowned in the process.

Ed said that he would prefer that there was a Tory government than do any sort of deal with the SNP. All over Scotland people were saying - did he say what I thought he said? Eh? Did that actually happen there? Noooo. Here put that telly on rewind and let me hear that bit again. Well in the name of the wee man. He did so. He did so say that. The last remnants of Labour support shrivelled and died from shame and embarrassment and the twitter trolls retreated under their bridge just as the bridge collapsed. Labour's last supporters fell silent and you could hear a feather drip canal watter. Vote Labour or Ed and the Labour party will make damn sure you get the Tories to punish you for daring to think for yourself. And you thought extortion was illegal.

He did try to backtrack a bit, and if you looked at the fine print he hadn't actually ruled out anything much. The SNP have already ruled out a coalition, Ed has now ruled out a confidence and supply deal. So we are left with the possibility of a minority government where Labour has to try and pass more than gall stones, and it can only do that by not pissing off other parties whose support it's going to need. So not off to a good start then. Labour doesn't know how to share.

But there was no doubt about the sentiment - one shared by all three party leaders - Scotland isn't welcome in the Union if it doesn't behave itself and vote the way Westminster wants. So there you have it. Remember all that guff last year about families of nations and Scotland punching above its weight and being valued and loved? Remember Ed telling us that if he was Prime Minister he'd give Scotland home rule? Ed Miliband is still more afraid of the Tory press than he is of five million pissed off Scottish people. It's up to us now to show him who he really needs to be scared of.

The Union is a dead parrot, and it's blue.

**Greetin Wee Weans**

*2 May 2015*

Ed Miliband, the guy threatening to disembowel himself with a rolled up copy of the Daily Mail if Scotland votes SNP, came on a visit to Glasgow on Friday. It was a desperate attempt to shore up the rapidly collapsing dam holding up the Labour vote in Scotland, despite the fact that Ed has taken his finger out the dyke and then attacked it with a pneumatic drill. Perhaps that explains why Ed holds his hands in interviews like he's slammed his fingers in the door.

Before the usual Labour mass rally - that's the special Labour definition of mass rally, a small group of invited Labour party activists and the press - Ed gave a speech while outside protesters played the theme song to the Muppet Show. Which was unfair on the Muppets. Although like Labour their glory days are long in the past, the Muppets are actually remembered with affection and do still have fans that don't work for them.

Ed wants us to think about our grandparents and how they would have voted and cast our vote accordingly. My late grandmother was a racist auld bigot who thought that African people rejected the Empire out of sheer pig headed ungratefulness. While Ed is certainly not a racist, I suspect that his understanding of why Scots are rejecting the Labour party is about as sophisticated as my grandmother's understanding of colonialism in mid 20th century Africa.

Some in the party have a more Victorian understanding. Jack McConnell, the man they call Joke for a reason, told the Guardian that even if the combined number of Labour and SNP MPs is greater, if the Tories are larger than Labour then Labour would have to allow Cameron to form a government. Jack thinks making statements like this are helpful to Labour in Scotland. No, really. If the natives don't do what the colonial governors want, they must be punished. If Labour and the SNP combined do form a majority in the Commons after Thursday's vote, Jack's comments will be repeated ad nauseam in the Tory press along with similar comments from Jim Murphy. But then the bitter-enders of Scottish Labour and their South African educated leader are willing to destroy Ed's chances of replacing the Tories in their pathetic attempts to cling onto their own privilege and preference.

But Labour has let out a collective sigh of relief because the telly has forgotten there's an election on because Willnkate had a baby. You may have noticed. Mostly the nation was grateful and happy because it meant that Nicholas Witchell could piss off and go home. Nicholas practically had an orgasm on the BBC news, so thrilled was he to be the centre of attention again. When there are no Royal events going on, Nicholas is kept in a coffin in the basement of Broadcasting House where he's kept alive on a drip feeding him Royal Wedding memorabilia that's been put through a blender.

The new Royal baby can't be leapfrogged, said Nicholas, breathlessly reporting from his fire escape, as though the Windsors were world leaders in the struggle for women's rights. A tiny rich minority who are handed privilege on a plate because they have a penis will be joined by a tiny rich minority who are handed privilege on a plate because they have a vagina. So no leapfrogging there then. The new Royal Succession Act doesn't mention anything about swings and roundabouts.

Nicholas has been standing outside that hospital doorway for weeks now, but they're still not letting him in. He's wearing a pink and blue tie, which is the BBC's definition of unbiased. Poor Nick has to stand outside with the red white and blue bedecked obsessives that he struggles not to call fans or stalkers, while telling us that this is a really private moment for Willnkate that's receiving 24 hour rolling news coverage. Some of these people have a fashion sense that make Orange marchers look tasteful and understated. Some even have boas like the one their father woa.

Over on Sky, his drag act equivalent Kay Burley was dangerously close to exploding. She keeps telling us how quickly it all happened, and you can sense her immense disappointment because she had been expecting to milk this for hours, if not days. This has taken us all by surprise says Kay, because Kay wasn't paying attention in sex-ed classes at school and didn't realise that pregnant women give birth.

Both Nicholas and Kay were gushing and hyperventilating to such an extent I was waiting for the security services to rush over at any moment and surround the pair of them with yellow tape before fingering them with a robot and then blowing them up safely. I would actually watch that. Hell, I'd pay to watch that.

Now there's frantic speculation about what the sprog is going to be called. David Cameron reportedly wants them to call her Nicola in the hope that it might persuade Scotland that the UK loves us. She won't be called Nicola after Nicholas Witchell, if she was named after Nicholas Witchell they'd have to call her Sycophancia, and that would be cruel. Others say the wean will be called Margaret Rose after the Queen's sister, because the child can be given a role model by naming her after a gin-soaked wastrel who never did anything useful her entire life. Although to be fair, that's a good description of the entire Royal family.

Attention then turns to how the new sprog's brother will take the news. That's easy enough to answer, he'll act like a small toddler. Which is exactly how the UK media has been reacting to the news too, complete with wetting itself. Actually, that's pretty much how the Labour party and the UK media have been reacting to the prominence of Scotland and the rise of the SNP in the General Election as well - with jealousy, stamping of feet and temper tantrums and throwing its toys out of the pram.

An aged and demented political party dies after succumbing to the sclerosis of the British establishment, and TV news greets the birth of an aristocrat who is a part of the British establishment from day one. That sums up where the UK is going, and why it's in desperate need of reform. We need to vote for real change on Thursday. Let's make them greet like wee weans.

## Edhenge

*3 May 2015*

I t's the final straight before the big vote, and Ed Miliband is channelling Spinal Tap and has turned the dial up to 11. He's even got something to offer literalists who struggle with the concept of metaphor. Hell yeah it's set in stone. He's promised that if he's elected he'll commission a big structure with Labour's manifesto promises carved into stone, which he'll erect in the rose gardens at the back of 10 Downing Street. Ed's wee spinning munchkins will dance around it while crooning his greatest hit - It's my party and I'll lie if I want to. It's going to be a permanent symbol of Ed's commitment to cheap publicity stunts which achieve precisely nothing. So pretty much like the last Labour government then.

It's the perfect symbol of the modern UK and what the welcoming place has become - a massive stone face bearing the legend Controls on Immigration. But of course it's really a tombstone representing the death of common sense and decency, although they died in the Labour party a very long time ago.

Most people would settle for a potting shed or garden gnomes, but not Ed. Labour has already got lots of small tasteless plastic people. But it is a shame that the idea was ruled out as it would kill two birds with one stone, many of them will be redundant by the end of the week and they could take up a productive career as a blight on Ed's garden instead of a blight on Scottish public life. Magrit Curran could sit with a wee plastic pole and fish for her expenses. The great thing about garden gnomes is that they never catch anything and have to sit motionless and silent. So there's already three reasons why we'd love Magrit to take the gig.

Ed said that the stone would symbolise his commitment to keep his pledges and rebuild trust in British politics, a bit like Rory the Tory's big pile of chucky stanes which was supposed to symbolise the eternal union between our two blesséd countries and which promptly vanished as soon as the independence referendum was out of the way. We can trust that Ed's big stane will be equally irrelevant and impermanent, and within a week of the election it will be tied around the feet of the party's Scottish strategists as they are tossed off the Labour boat as the recriminations get into full swing.

It's very much in the tradition of Labour statements, presented in private before selected and invitation only audiences in venues that are not accessible to the general public. Only this time it's in stone. It's Edhenge, a big thick stone faced waste of space - a sort of Gordon Brown without any moving parts or expensive expenses claims, but about as sentient.

Sadly Edhenge won't be coming with an altar stone upon which Jim Murphy can be disembowelled by the druid Iandavidsonix as a sacrifice to Shallogimmix, the

Celtic god of Labour manifesto commitments and publicity stunts. Ian has already volunteered for the job, because Labour likes to get its infighting started early. I might have voted for that. But not to worry, the Labour party is doing a sterling job of bayonetting itself and Jim without any assistance. Originally the plan called for them to build a wicker man and stuff it full of straw, before setting fire to it and allowing it to combust in a bonfire of its own vanity, but they've already got Anas Sarwar as a vain self-regarding straw man whose career is in ashes, so it was deemed superfluous.

Edhenge is all a bit grandiose and over-compensatory for a man who struggled with a bacon sandwich. Just because it's a big heavy lump doesn't mean it's got gravitas Ed. You can't manufacture political solidity, you can't fake sincerity. If Ed had really wanted a garden monument to keep him on his toes and not just some cheap publicity stunt that would generate a photo opportunity, he could have promised that he'd dig up the Downing Street rose garden and turn it into vegetable allotments to remind him that there are people in this country who can't feed themselves and who have to rely on food banks because of government policies. If Ed really did have gravitas and sincerity he could have sworn that he'd only allow the roses to return once food banks had been abolished and that in the meantime he'd be spending all his working time working to abolish them, and all his spare time down on the allotment growing potatoes.

Ed is King Milibandias, look on his works ye mighty and giggle uncontrollably for a bit. The technical term for a useless hunk of stone that you plonk in your garden for decorative purposes is a folly. And a monumental folly is also a good description of Ed's electoral strategy and his decision to tell Scotland and Wales that their votes only count if they vote for Westminster approved parties - otherwise he's going to let the Tories get into power. Who is advising this clown?

Seriously. Ed Miliband is surrounded by people who thought this was a good idea, and not one of them thought to say "You do realise this is going to make us look like total idiots, don't you?" Not one. And we're supposed to trust this guy's judgement?

Possibly the big stick of Edhenge rock is intended to be one of the obelisks from 2001, and its mere presence will impart sentience upon the rock bangers and head bangers surrounding it who will rapidly evolve into self-aware beings. It will certainly raise the average IQ of the advisors who thought it was a good idea.

But it's far too late for Labour to evolve into intelligent life, and Labour self-awareness died the day that they elected Tony Blair as party leader. On the eve of an election - they commission a tombstone. That's the only symbolism that people will take from this latest idiocy.

Labour may be building a tombstone for itself, but its death will still go unmourned.

## Just Another Manic Fundilymundily

*4 May 2015*

Following from a disastrous weekend, Jim Murphy has had a manic fundilymundily. On one of his megaphonic irn bru crate assisted standabouts in Glasgow, yelling at passers-by who don't give a toss, he was met by an equally small group of independence supporters yelling at Labour politicians and activists who don't give a toss either. And Eddie Izzard was there too, for extra glam and star appeal. Although for some bizarre reason Eddie thought that extra glam meant doing what was, to be fair, a pretty good impression of Johann Lamont. Some handbags were drawn at dawn - or at least before noon - there was allegedly a bit of shoving, there was definitely a spot of yelling, and it was the Smugurph's egg moment all over again, this time with lipstick. Help help, Jim's being oppressed and underdoggy. Vote for him out of sympathy.

How very dare the punters not stand in silent reverence to listen to the words of the Rev Jim, for Jim preacheth the path to salvation. At least the salvation of his career. Indeed, in the last few days of the campaign saving Jim's career is what Labour is all about. Jim and Wee Dougie and Magrit. The rest of the Labour party is being left to its own devices. This is why Jim has been banging on about another fundilymundily referendum, he's hoping to attract the support of Tory voters in the Mearns. Only the Tories can save Jim now. Jim doesn't do irony, so it's just as well that the rest of us do.

But instead of quiet reverence and grateful oohs at how convincing Eddie is at impersonating Johann, there was carnage. This is what happens when people stop listening to Labour you know, the very fabric of the universe unravels and chaos results. 30 Labour activists and four protesters are capable of bringing civilisation to its knees. Jim is all that stands between Scotland and the ravenous horde of a campaigner seeking a Subway moment. Although he did bugger off in a car as soon as the telly cameras had got some close up photies to make the crowd look bigger than it really was. So he didn't do that much standing up. Jim's job is done as soon as the BBC cameraman says it's a wrap. And not the sort of wrap you get in Subway.

Jim was delighted as it distracted attention from the fact he was fundilymundily humiliated by Ruth Davidson in Sunday's debate. The Action Krankie prefaced her remarks with an apology for being about to use unparliamentary language, and all over Scotland ears pricked up in the eager anticipation that Ruthie was about to call Jim a dickhead. But as it turned out she only called him a liar to his face. Which is just fair comment and considerably milder than what everyone else calls him, and all across Scotland ears sagged and people went "Och, is that it."

"How very dare you," replied Jim, offended that someone had said out loud what everyone has been thinking for years, like a man with a bad toupee who's just been told that he's wearing a lovely hat. Although he was even more offended that the Tory voters in the Mearns might be listening to Ruthie and not to him.

However the real highlight of the debate was Jim's invention of a new word, no one is very sure what the word means, and no one cares. Very little that Jim says makes any sense anyway, but for the first time in his career Labour's branch officer manager has actually made a positive contribution to Scottish public life. But by fundilymundily all was forgotten as the telly moved on to carnage rioting and outrage. Some Glaswegian people got shouty, and this is news. And, brace yourself, someone dropped a placard. No really. That's littering that is, and that's a crime. It's a national disgrace.

It was Sean Clerkin who was giving Jim a run for his expenses claims in the shouty department. It is news that Sean Clerkin is shouty like it's news that the Kardashians are botoxified attention seekers. Sean is indeed the Khloe Kardashian of the independence movement. Sean is best known, indeed is only known, for his confrontation of Iain Gray in a Subway sandwich shop in 2011. In an attempt at a sequel, Sean decided to confront Jim Murphy outside a subway station, megamouth to megamouth. Sean has also done his shouty demonstrating thing against the SNP, with whom he's had a number of run ins. This won't prevent the UK media from demanding that Nicola apologise for his behaviour.

According to the BBC, a minor outbreak of subrammyness, far less threatening than the scenes you'll see outside just about every nightclub in the city on a Saturday night, was "absolute chaos on the streets of Glasgow". This is the very same broadcaster which saw fit to describe the real violence and assaults perpetrated on Yes campaigners by baying Unionist mobs of fascists as "disturbances". So not absolutely chaotic then.

However fundilymundily's rammyette, according to the Scottish media, eagerly seeking something to discredit the evil nationalists, was the worst outbreak of street violence since the Siege of Constantinople in 1453. That one saw the collapse of a civilisation as well, although to be honest, describing the Labour party in Scotland as civilised is a bit of a stretch. Admittedly, so is describing them as sentient.

There has been a depressing litany of bad behaviour on the part of Unionists, bad behaviour which has actually resulted in real violence, court cases and convictions. There has been nothing comparable from the nasty nats. Yet the media focusses almost exclusively on the shoutiness of only one side, and it's not the ones with a real track record of violence or spouting hatred. That's what happens when an establishment is under threat, it lashes out, but its lashing out is entirely reasonable because the establishment - by definition - takes it upon itself to define what is or is not reasonable. In a desperate attempt to save themselves they're trying to re-run the referendum campaign and whip up a few Tories to save Jim's skin.

It's not going to work, the establishment's fundilymundily days are numbered.

## For the Record

*5 May 2015*

We all know that the traditional Scottish media is pants, and the Daily Record is the skidmarks. Today on page 10 the paper published a wee moany press release by Magrit Curran - the dangleberry of the Labour party - about a short piece I'd written in support of Natalie McGarry who is standing against Magrit in Glasgow East.

The paper did not see fit to contact me about the story, and describes me as "an SNP blogger". This is incorrect - as I have said on this blog on numerous occasions previously, I am not an SNP member and do not write at the behest of the SNP. I wrote the piece in a personal capacity. If the Record had seen fit to engage in the most fundilymundily journalism and contacted me instead of printing a Labour press release verbatim, they'd have known that. Och, journalism and the Daily Record, what am I thinking? Still, it's hugely pleasing to know that I'm getting under Magrit's skin, an enormous delight to discover that my words wound her.

Magrit thinks my words are patronising and insulting to the people of Glasgow East. Coming from a woman who has spent her entire career patronising and insulting the intelligence of the people of Glasgow East, and the rest of Scotland, this is pretty rich. But before going on to patronise and insult Magrit, here's the piece I wrote for Natalie. You can judge for yourselves.

*We have a choice before us with this election. Walk down Shettleston Road, take a stroll through Tollcross Park, and you can see the drawn faces of a people who have been abandoned, betrayed by those for whom aspiration means leaving Glasgow East behind, a place to be from not a place to be a part of. One choice is passivity, we can choose to sit back and bemoan the fact that Glasgow East is known for low life expectancy, for poverty, for substance abuse, for multiple social deprivation.*

*Passivity means that we can vote as we've always done, as our grandparents did, and sit back in hopelessness and despair, lost amongst the drawn faces in Tollcross Park - or we can choose to stand tall and shout. We can demand. We can choose to make our vibrant voices heard, we can choose to be loud, to be gallus. We can choose to be the proud grandchildren of those who created a movement for change, a force for social justice. And we can choose to do that again.*

*Here and now, we can start to create a future our grandchildren can be proud of, and Natalie McGarry is the woman who will be the voice of that future.*

*Not all politicians are the same. Natalie McGarry's aspiration is be a part of this community, to be of it not from it, to carry its message to the corridors of power, to speak truth and be an agent of change, an agent of social justice.*

*This is a time for change. This is a time for making a difference. This is a time for grasping the thistle of the future. Be the change, be the difference, make the future. Scotland's future rests in your hands, in your vote and voice. Be active, be a force, be a strong voice.*

*Dare to hope.*

*Vote SNP, vote for Natalie McGarry.*

Magrit thinks it's insulting and patronising to point out that people who suffer the effects of her misrule and the misrule of the Tories are pained and damaged because of it. She's the one who campaigned in order to keep Scotland at risk of Tory rule, she's the one who danced and clapped as Davie Cameron prepared his EVEL speech.

Running to the Record to complain about my words is a sign of her pathetic desperation, a risible attempt to manufacture sympathy for herself on the backs of those whose benefits have been sanctioned, who walk the cold and hungry miles to a food bank, who wrap themselves in blankets because they have no money for the meter. Those are the people Magrit should be fighting for, but no, she'd rather complain to the Record that someone from her own constituency, someone who unlike her actually lives in the East End, has dared to point them out to her. That's why Magrit is a hypocrite. Away with you Magrit, back to yer big hoose in Newlands.

Magrit says that the people of the East End need hope. She says I insult them. How dare you speak to us about hope. We do have hope for the future Magrit. We are hopeful of a future that doesn't have you in it. You are a barrier to progress, a blockage that needs to be flushed out and flushed away. You are the voice of a sclerotic establishment that promises a privatised sticking plaster on the gaping wounds of a community whose soul your party has ripped out.

But now the pressure is rising. Magrit can feel it, she can feel it about to burst and take her career with it. So she runs to the Record with her whiny press releases. And when Magrit is flushed away the cheers from Glasgow East will be heard all the way to Westminster. No one here wants you Magrit. You can trust me on that one. I live in Glasgow East, you don't. I talk to real people who live here, you live in the manufactured bubble of press releases and media events attended only by party hacks. You know nothing Magrit, but even you in your place of ignorance can feel the tremors of the earthquake that's coming.

Magrit's panicking now, and in her panic she reveals herself as a woman bereft of poetry, absent from any finer feeling, lacking in compassion, and a stranger to the truth. The only thing Magrit has ever felt any passion for is her expenses claims and her public standing. We're going to take those things from her.

It's not that the blood is slowly dripping out of Magrit's career, it's spurting from the jugular and she's drowning in it. Tick tock Magrit, just two days to go. The pale and drawn face will be yours. The lost and lonely figure will be yours. Focus group that.

You'll have many years ahead of you to enjoy your obscurity Magrit. But you won't enjoy it anything like as much as we will.

## Making a Vow

*6 May 2015*

Well here we are. It's been a long slog, but at last the Jockalypse day of judgement has arrived and we get to send the Unionist parties a message that they can't miss. This time the message needs to be the last post.

Politicians are always waffling on about messages, but the best message to give them is a kick in the nads and to separate them from their cushy careers and their expense accounts. Get them where it hurts. If each of us had a penny for every time that a Labour careerist had told us their party was listening and changing there would be nae bloody national deficit and we wouldn't be in the mess we're in now.

We've heard it all before. Scotland keeps sending messages to the Labour party. 2007, 2011, and every time it was the same. Labour was listening. Magrit Curran would write a report that never saw the light of day. The party would have a period of reflection. The problem is that the Labour party thinks a period of reflection means looking at themselves in a mirror and telling themselves they've still got it, that they're still sexy, like a middle aged man holding in his beer belly and carefully combing his hair to cover up the bald spot.

Then Labour decided that the solution to the problem was to give us more of the problem, and elected Jim Murphy as leader. Presumably on the principle that if you're in a hole what you really need isn't a ladder it's a JCB. Jim, a man who thinks integrity is a description of stone chipping. Shonky fly by night cowboys who turn up on your doorstep offering to relay your driveway have more integrity than Jim. If he does manage to save his own seat, he'll do so on the back of Tory votes. Tories feel comfortable with Jim. That tells us all we need to know about Jim and his approach to politics.

Thursday is the day when we get to tell the Labour that they're not god's gift to political gorgeousness. They're clapped out moronic rip off merchants, long past their sell by date, a mugging dressed as bams. Sexysocialism is to be found elsewhere. Labour is not a party its founders would recognise however much it tries to claim the mantle of Scottish radicalism. Labour betrayed that heritage and turned its back on it, turned its back on the communities that gave birth to it. It's trading on a false prospectus, offering to relay our driveway.

Labour needs to go. It acts as a barrier to progress, a blockage in the way of Scottish self-government, because when faced with a choice between what Scotland wants and what's good for the Labour party, Labour always chooses the second. Always. It's the only principle they've got. Labour thinks it is the people's party and so whatever it says or does is for the people. But the people have walked away. The people no longer want to know. Labour is left squawking alone like an unwashed bampot with a shopping trolley shouting abuse at a phone box, an embarrassment that we quickly walk by without eye contact.

The clock is also ticking on the Lib Dems, the Tory enablers, the draculettes. Many of those who voted for them last time did so in order to keep the Tories out - and look what the party did next. Going back on their promise to resist student fees was a minor betrayal by comparison. Danny Alexander acceded to the post of George Osborne's little minion with an unseemly pleasure, more Tory than the Tories themselves.

The clock was also supposed to be ticking on the report into the Frenchgate leak - remember we were supposed to get the results of that before the election? That's an alarm that has remained strangely silent. Funny that. It may yet save Alistair Carmichael's koala arse.

This is the election where the main Westminster parties have done their utmost to keep the punters out of politics. We've seen one carefully staged press event after another. We've had the farce of a so-called people's party holding meetings and not inviting the people. All of them, Labour, the Tories and the Lib Dems, all of them tell us with their carefully staged press events that we are not invited to the party. Vote for us, they say, and you can stand on the outside with your nose pressed against the window. Vote to be excluded. Vote to be shut out. Vote to be held at arm's length.

Why should we trust a political party with our futures when it won't even trust us to be in the same room as its representatives? Why are they surprised that we are turning en masse to the only main party which actually welcomes the company of ordinary people? The contrast between Labour and the SNP has been striking. One goes out into the streets and meets the people, the other hides behind closed doors and relies on its friends in the press.

On voting day Scotland has its second date with destiny within the space of a year. This time it's personal. This time we have the opportunity to show the Westminster parties that when they promised real change in the final days of the referendum campaign, a No vote did not mean they could return to short-changing us. They forgot that they are supposed to do as we say, and in their power and arrogance came to believe that we should do as they tell us. They are not the power in this land - that would be us, those of us who don't get invited to the carefully orchestrated press events. It would be those of us who Magrit Curran didn't speak to when she wrote one of her Labour party reports.

Let's make a vow of our own. Let's vow that henceforth we will not be taken for granted. Let's vow to eject those who have let us down. Let's vow to teach Labour what pandafication means. Let's vow to make Scotland's voice heard loud in the corridors of power. Let's vow to be the power in this land.

## Oh What a Night

*8 May 2015*

Well that was some night. So you know how we're supposed to be gracious and generous in victory? How we should be mature adults, be bigger people than the small minded pursed lippy types of Labour? Well fuck that. Hahahahahahahahaha... and breathe... hahahahaha. Get it right up yese ya pandaficated basterts.

Phew, now I've got that off my chest I'd like to apologise to people in the east of Glasgow and North Lanarkshire for the sonic boom which rattled your windows at about 3.30 am. That was me and the dug cheering when Magrit Curran lost her seat. In the end the Cuban cigar with which I had intended to celebrate the defeat of La Curran was not a success. I had one puff, and felt dizzy, light headed, and very nauseous. Which was probably pretty much how Magrit was feeling at that moment too. She was being turned to ash as well. So I dumped it in the bin and it's now en route to the dump along with Magrit's career. Neither will be missed.

Magrit didn't just lose, she was Fukushima'd - there was a tsunami, a melt down and then she got pumped. I hope she got some boxes of Kleenex on expenses before she

112

lost her seat, she's going to need them. The SNP candidate Natalie McGarry obtained 57% of all the votes cast and won a majority of 10,000. Magrit's career is now as dead as Labour's socialism.

I honestly thought Jim Murphy would hold on to his seat, I thought that the Tories in the Mearns would have been quite comfortable voting for a capitalist war-mongerer who loves privatisation and student fees. But he was too right wing even for them.

Despite losing his seat to a Kirsten Oswald who skooshed to victory with more grace than a chancer on an Irn Bru crate could ever muster, Jim Murphy is still clinging on to the job of Labour branch office manager like a tapeworm in the party's colon. Taking responsibility is only for people who are below Jim's pay grade. It's going to take more than utter obliteration to evict Jim. You know how thon advert for bleach says it kills 99% of all germs dead, well Jim is the 1%, and it's the 1% that he represents politically too.

Jim is like one of those wee mutant beasties that survive even a nuclear war of an electoral wipe-out. His survival is down to sheer pig headed refusal to accept reality which is due to the fact that Jim has spent his career living in a self-generated media bubble telling him how invaluable he is. He's never had a job in his entire life and it's unreasonable of us to expect him to get one now, although you'd think he'd be happy that he's now got time to finish that degree course. Although it's cruel of me to say that, as now he's lost his job and his expense account he can't afford the student fees.

Labour is too shell shocked by the magnitude of their defeat to consider challenging Jim - for now. They're too deep in shock to face up to the truth that they have a branch office manager who managed to lose 97% of their Westminster seats. That's failure on a truly epic scale. But even if they did decide to challenge him, who have they got? Kezia Dugdale? After a defeat like this Labour in Scotland needs to think very seriously about whether they have a future as a part of British Labour. Labour in Scotland needs to grow up and become a Scottish party.

Scotland now has more Trident subs than pro-Trident MPs. Even the sole remaining Labour MP owes a large part of his survival to his open opposition to Trident renewal. He owes an even greater part to the campaign of vilification and lies undertaken by the Scottish media against his opponent. But it can't be argued that Ian Murray was definitely on the left of the Labour party. The SNP is unquestionably to the left of the Labour party. So is Labour still going to claim that Scotland isn't really a more left wing country than England? Probably.

Labour blames the SNP for its defeat. The Unionist parties went around screaming to anyone who would listen - which would be the BBC and Fleet Street - that the SNP would eat your babies. Labour smiled indulgently on the antics of Ian Smart when he called the SNP fascists and supporters of the Nazis. Labour looked upon a mildly left of centre social democratic party and it saw a scary monster. Then they blamed the SNP because voters in England were afraid of the imaginary monster that Labour had invented.

The Tories have already begun to speak openly of things they didn't dare mention when they didn't expect to get an absolute majority. The Telegraph has already called for the NHS to be funded by a private insurance system, Theresa May has already announced plans for a snooper's charter. We're facing billions of pounds in cuts to benefits for the poor, the disabled and the vulnerable. The only boom we'll see is in the number of food banks.

Cameron says he's going to govern as if the UK were one nation. Which basically means he's going to ignore Scotland and pretend that we don't exist. No matter how bad you feel that we've got another five years of Tory rule ahead of us, just think how much worse you'd be feeling if we'd voted Labour and were faced with fifty expenses claimants who'd put party before country. But instead we've got 56 SNP MPs, the Scottish unicorn has stuck its horn right up the arse of the British establishment. They're not sitting comfortably. They will not be able to ignore us ever again.

The task of the 56 SNP MPs will be to twist the unicorn's horn ever deeper into the flesh of the British establishment. Their job is to remind us that there is another way. There is another vision. We must grasp the thistle of the future and have confidence in ourselves. With last night's result, Scotland's independence just got closer.

## The Govefish and the Baurheid Doo

*10 May 2015*

It's Sunday, and Jim Murphy still hasn't resigned. The half of Scotland who voted SNP on Thursday wants Jim to remain in post. Jim lost over 97% of Labour's MPs, he could still repeat the trick with their MSPs next year. You'd think the Labour party in Scotland would have got rid of him by now, being tipped off by the fact that SNP supporters are so keen for Jim to stay, but Strathclyde Uni's least successful student is still Labour's Scottish branch manager even though one unnamed MSP told the Sunday Herald that Jim is as popular as herpes.

There is no cure for herpes, and it seems there is no cure for Jim either. There's nothing in the rules of the Labour party that gives the other members the right to evict him. Labour's increasingly desperate MSPs and cooncillors must rely on Jim's grace and statesmanlike sense of personal responsibility to fall on his sword and resign for leading the party into its worst result since 1918. Now there's a laugh. Jim Murphy and statesmanlike are two concepts that only ever appear in the same sentence if there's a negative in there somewhere - like that negative there.

Jim Murphy's like the office manager in the Full Monty who was too afraid to tell his wife he'd been made redundant, so he got up every day, put on a suit and took his sandwiches to a park bench where he managed the doos. As I type this, Jim is sitting on a park bench in Baurheid, telling the doos about his plans for a Labour recovery. I can still be First Minister you know, he told a particularly scabrous and vicious doo he mistook for John McTernan after it crapped on his head.

While all this is going on, Jim's bosses dahn sarf are concluding that Labour's problem was that it was trying to be too cuddly and compassionate and in fact if the party wants to be re-elected they really need to be more Tory. Which means in turn that they've pretty much abandoned Scotland. The only hope for Labour in Scotland now is for them to secede from UK Labour and become a properly Scottish party. There's a delicious irony, Labour in Scotland fought for a No result in the referendum and will end up having to declare its own independence because of it.

But Scotland has more serious problems than the light comedy relief of Jim's and the Labour party's self-inflicted predicament. We're faced with a right wing Tory government far more vicious than any Baurheid doo, and it's going to crap on the heads of the poor and the vulnerable from a great height. Moreover this Tory government got into power in part by demonising Scotland as well as the usual suspects - the poor, the EU, and migrants.

Speaking on a personal level, as a gay man I was demonised by the Tory party in the 1980s during the Thatcher era, so am thrilled that as a Scot living in an era when gay rights are accepted as the norm that I've still got some of that demonic mojo going for me. Because let's be honest here, if you scare the shiters out of the Tories, you must be doing something right. And now I've got all 5 million of you for company.

The Tory attack on civil liberties has already started. Theresa May remains as Home Secretary. She's the woman who said that Scotland voting SNP would provoke the greatest crisis since the abdication and instead provoked the greatest outbreak of ridicule in the history of Twitter. She has introduced plans for a snoopers' charter, allowing the security services access to emails and social media information. Nicky Morgan, who voted against gay marriage, is Equalities Minister. They keep telling us that irony is supposed to be a British virtue, but the Tories show no sign of comprehending it.

Meanwhile Michael Gove, half man half goldfish, has been appointed as the new Secretary of State for Justice. Gove had to flee from his native Aberdeen to Safetoryseatshire in England on account of the fact that even the Tory party in Scotland thought he was unelectable and was polluting the water of their goldfish bowl. Although to be fair, they're pretty unelectable themselves. Despite the Action Krankie supposedly having a great election campaign, she saw a drop in the Tory vote to a mere 14.9%. So not that great a campaign. More tanks and Soleros next time then Ruth.

The Govefish is a man who argued that abolishing hanging was a bad idea, criticised the investigation into police failings during the Stephen Lawrence murder investigation, and didn't want an enquiry into Westminster paedophiles. Now he's charged with abolishing the Human Rights Act and replacing it with some hauf-airsed "British Bill of Rights", which you can be sure will take rights away from you and give them to your boss and to the state. Thankfully Michael Gove won't be responsible for justice in Scotland, he will just be responsible for injustice throughout the UK.

The Scottish Government is obliged to comply with European Human Rights law, and human rights are devolved. According to legal blogger Lallands Peat Worrier, the Human Rights Act itself isn't enshrined in the Scotland Act, but there are numerous legal strands connecting Scottish devolution with human rights legislation. Even with the active cooperation of the Scottish Government the Tories would find it neither easy nor straightforward to disentangle them, but there will be no cooperation, Cameron's new British rights for British mince will run into the implacable opposition of a Scottish Parliament which will not roll over and allow the Tories to run roughshod over Scots law and an SNP which now has representation on every Commons committee. A legal mess is looming.

This is how the UK will end, amidst confusion and legal disputes as the Tories discover that the irresistible force of Westminster parliamentary sovereignty runs into the immovable object of Scottish popular sovereignty. Westminster says that parliament is sovereign and it can do as it pleases, meanwhile Scotland says that the people are sovereign and Westminster can bugger off. It's going to be a rocky ride and we're in for a whole lot more crap than can be produced by even the most scabrous Baurheid doo.

## Skooshing Away from the Stuffed Panda Tea Party

*11 May 2015*

Davie Cameron has told us that we're not going to be allowed to have another independence referendum. The wee sowel thinks it's up to him to decide whether we can or not, bless. We'll tell you when we're going to have another indyref Davie son, we don't need your permission. At a Scottish Parliament election, if Scotland votes for a party with an independence referendum in its manifesto, we'll have an independence referendum. That's how this democracy thing works, although you can appreciate that an upper class Etonian Tory might struggle with the concept.

Of course, we're not going to have another independence referendum for the time being. That would be silly. We had one of those last year, and we lost it. Scotland's voters know that. We also know that we won't be having another indyref until we know we're going to win independence, and the rate at Davie Cameron is getting up the collective nostrils of the Scottish public that could be next week. In fact, if Iain Duncan Smith opens his gob before the end of the day, it could very well be tomorrow.

Oh but what about respecting the will of the 55% who voted No, the Unionists cry. Although in the case of the

Labour party and the Lib Dems it's hard to distinguish that crying from the crying they're doing because they've been wiped out.

But that's the point isn't it - there will be no second independence referendum until the 55% is no longer a 55%, so there won't be any 55% majority whose views demand respect. It's arguable whether there is still a 55% in any case. According to opinion polls the 55% is now more like a 51%, which works out at a loss in Unionist support of 0.5% every month. If that rate of attrition is maintained by the time of the Scottish elections next year 57% of Scotland's voters will be supporting independence. And that's without the accelerant factor of a majority Tory government to piss us all off even more.

If there's one thing we've learned about the clueless vicious ineptitude of majority Tory governments, they're world class experts in pissing off people in Scotland. They've already done it some more with Cameron's announcement about no more independence referendums. Cameron has no right to speak for Scotland, he hasn't noticed that a Mundell isn't a mandate. A mundell is a small stuffed toy bear, although that's being terribly cruel to the intellectual capabilities of sawdust filled pandas, which are actually capable of attending a dolls' tea party without adult supervision.

The sawdust filled panda is the new Secretary of State for Scotland, taking over from the sawdust filled koalamichael. And all of Scotland went "Ooooh that's a surprise," in a heavily sarcastic tone. This is the panda that said just a wee while back that the post of Secretary of State was "above his pay grade". Asking Scotland if it wants to make that a supersized meal is above the stuffed panda's pay grade. But it's not like Davie Cameron was terribly spoiled for choice.

Meanwhile the funerals are in full swing over at Labour towers. Perhaps I should stop slagging off the Labour party in Scotland, because it's wrong to speak ill of the dead, but Jim Murphy is still infesting the corpse. Just thought I'd put that out there, because Labour still isn't putting Jim out. We need as many strong anti-Tory voices as we can get right now Labour party in Scotland - and you lot aren't helping. Get your collective finger out of your collective arse, and stop feeling sorry for yourselves. Try and remember that the reason we all hate you is because you are a bunch of useless self-serving wastes of space, and continuing to be a bunch of useless self-serving wastes of space isn't helping your case any.

Labour can start by getting rid of Jim, and then maybe, just maybe, they can start doing what they were supposed to be doing in the first place - being a voice for the people of Scotland. It should be too difficult, because SLab has only got one voice now, that would be Ian Murray the Shadow Secretary of State for Union Jackets. Labour isn't terribly spoiled for choice either.

But Labour won't be escaping popular ire any time soon. The party south of the border seems to have decided that it lost the election because it wasn't Blairite enough. Because what we really need in order to achieve social justice and equality is a party that's in favour of Iraqi wars, sooking up to Kazakhstani dictators and being indistinguishable from the Tories. Now we've got the arch Blairite Chuka Umunna making a pitch for the leadership, and rumours that the other Miliband will return from his self-imposed exile. The prince over the watter who will lead the party to another Scottish defeat because he'll speak down at us and not for us, not from amongst us.

And it's this rapidly diminishing set of choices that is driving the 55% on its ever downwards spiral and leading to the inevitable end of an unloved union. Scotland has become the colour blind person with discerning taste buds in the UK's political skoosh shop. Colour blind people can't tell the difference between orange coloured orange skoosh and green coloured lemon skoosh, both are thickly cloying and kill the sensitive tongue, the only difference is the chemical colourant. The Unionist media complains that with the rise of the SNP that Scotland is turning into a one party state, but the truth is that the UK became a one party state a long time ago, and the punters are offered a choice that's a non-choice between austerity loving neo-liberals who are distinguished only by their chemical additives. The flavour remains the same, and both of them equally rot your teeth and are bad for your health as they fill the cups in the dolly tea set at the stuffed panda party.

It's hardly surprising that Scotland is skooshing away after a different flavour of politics.

## The Prince Over the Twatter

*13 May 2015*

Not that anyone believed that the Royals were really politically neutral anyway. The only other institution which has an entire department of the BBC devoted to fawning over it is the Labour party in Scotland. They're deep in mourning over at Pacific Quay. Following the party's annihilation at the polls last week, rumour has it that John Boothman is writing letters in spindly black writing to government ministers asking for a state funeral to be presented by Nicholas Witchell.

The letters were all written between 2004 and 2005, when Alistair Darling was Scottish Secretary of State. But the Prince Over the Twatter didn't write to Alistair, he only wrote on topics he cares about, like Patagonian toothfish, the albatross around his neck, murdering badgers, and homoeopathic medicine. This tells us all we need to know about how much he cares about Scotland, but then he's not exactly Prince Popular here. Seems like the feeling is mutual. Alistair must have been gutted, because he's the brown noser's brown noser, and he positively leaps at the chance to fawn over arch Conservatives, as he proved at the Scottish Tory party conference.

The main thing to come out of these letters however is that they are very like the telly coverage of the Royal wedding or the birth of a Royal sprog. Deeply boring, narrow in focus, and entirely predictable, rather like the man himself. Shame really, because we were promised explosive revelations. The last time that a major hype failed to live up to expectations was Labour's election campaign. Possibly Jim Murphy's name was redacted from the Spider Memos. It would explain a lot.

Apart from telling us that we don't need no stinking badgers, another subject of immense concern to the man who talks to plants was the UK's sufficiency in vegetables. You'd think he only needed to look at his own courtiers and hangers on the realise there was no real shortage there. As long as we have a Royal family, the UK will never be short of brainless ornamental hardy perennials. We have Jim Murphy for that sort of thing too, although he's more of a persistent weed which you can't get rid of even after dousing East Renfrewshire with electoral paraquat.

We won't get to see any other letters written by Charles, or any other member of the Royal family, to the government. The government changed the law so that any letters from Royals are exempt from the Freedom of Information Act. The Royals have a legal right to lobby government ministers on any legislation which has an impact on their own interests, financial or otherwise. But we're not allowed to know about it. We just have to pay for it.

Right now there's a slew of bool moothed nonentities on the telly defending the right of Charles to write to the government in an attempt to get laws changed to suit himself or to tout for jobs for his pals. He's got just as much right to write to government ministers as anyone else, the bool mooths brown nose. Which must mean that any random punter who writes to a government minister about Nissen huts in Antarctica has an equal right to a detailed personally written and signed reply which covers every point raised in great detail and isn't just a form letter giving the brush off... Oh, wait.

The bool moothed ones tell us that the letters merely show how informed Charles is and how good it is that he's expressing concern. Which makes you wonder why successive governments fought toothfish and badger claw to keep them secret. They're simply the sort of concerns anyone who reads the Daily Telegraph or the Daily Mail might have, said a bool moothed type, answering the previous question. They're not the sort of concerns that anyone who reads more widely than the right wing press might have. The fact we're faced with a future head of state whose world view is determined by the contents of the Telegraph and the Mail is something of a worry, and not just if you're Scottish.

The bool moothed apologists have not noticed the irony that they're defending the supposed neutrality of British institution which is anything but neutral on the BBC, another British institution which is supposedly neutral but which isn't. We're living in Narnia, a land of make believe where story telling passes for news. And that's precisely why a significant number of us want independence - so we can live in a grown up country.

I want to live in a country where we don't have to fight long and expensive legal cases in order to discover what a future unelected head of state is lobbying for. I want to live in a country where the public broadcaster reflects the discussions and opinions of the public, it doesn't seek to form them or channel them in pre-approved directions.

We're stuck with Prince Charles, at least until independence, but we can do something about our other not so neutral British institution before that. Despite the many shortcomings and the obvious bias of the BBC's McTernan spider memos, we need a publicly funded broadcaster. The Tories are about to embark on an all-out assault on the principle of public funding for the BBC, and that's why we need to ensure that broadcasting is a devolved matter. Then we can have a public broadcaster that really does reflect the views of the Scottish public, and protect it from the Tories at the same time.

## The Secretary of State for Mundellirium

*14 May 2015*

We've got a new number two in the Scotland Office. And he is, by all accounts, a number two who has been dropped on the head of the Scottish body politic from a very great height. It's a bit of a surprise that the Tories have done it really, because being crap is about the only thing that David Mundell is capable of doing unassisted.

The new number two is Andrew Dunlop, who was an advisor to Thatcher when the poll tax was being devised and imposed on Scotland. Dunlop is reputedly one of those who were instrumental in creating the tax which made the Tories look like tools. Apart from starting the process which destroyed the Tory party in Scotland, Dunlop is best known for abusing his council car park pass to avoid paying £7.50 a day when he went off to London to advise Davie Cameron.

Davie chose him because he wanted someone with a tried and tested reputation in Scotland, but he couldn't have chosen anyone who had a lower standing in Scottish public opinion if he'd picked the Duke of Cumberland. Originally Davie had wanted to select the Duke, but was put off after discovering he's been dead a long time. A bit like the Tories in Scotland, come to think of it.

Dunlop is not an MP, and now Davie Cameron is giving him a peerage so he can impose even more unwanted Tory policies on Scotland all over again. Because that worked out so well for them the last time. But Davie Cameron, for reasons best known to himself, believes that the unelected Lord Placeperson of Patronageshire is exactly the guy who's needed to restore Scottish faith in the Westminster system. The Tories have already got a whole harrumph of out of touch Scottish Tories on the benches of the Lords, but it behoves the Cameron to create a new one, especially designed to get up the noses of Scottish opinion like a very persistent snotter that is out of reach of the most persistent digging finger. The Tories have clearly been taking lessons from the Labour party in Scotland in how to turn a deaf ear to Scottish public opinion.

Davie hopes that this will compensate for the mundellirium which will otherwise characterise Scottish Questions in the Commons, as even with the ritual SNP bashing non-questions from the red panda, the blue panda will be left stunned and confused by all the other Scottish MPs. To be honest, it's not difficult to stun and confuse David Mundell, who permanently bears the shocked and surprised expression of a man who's just realised that even though he is the last man on the planet, the last woman still won't touch him with a bargepole.

Giving us Thatcher's little minion to look over us is an example of Davie's respect agenda. People who are more in touch with Scottish opinion would call it a taking the piss agenda. But then Davie is so out of touch with Scottish opinion that even Jim Murphy is more in touch than Davie is, and Jim reads the Scottish runes in a basement illuminated by a burned out lightbulb and while he's wearing welding goggles. But Davie has a Tory majority and doesn't need to care what Scottish voters think, although if he thinks this appointment is going to help him save the Union he probably also believes that Katie Hopkins is an ideal choice for the post of United Nations High Commissioner for Refugees.

So the question is - in his handling of the Scottish question is Davie arrogant and high handed and annoying us all on purpose, or is he merely spectacularly stupid and ham fisted and making a number two situation even worse? Although it has to be said that those two propositions are not necessarily mutually exclusive. In fact, given an examination of Davie's previous incursions into Scottish affairs, it's a running certainty that they're both equally true.

We're getting another incursion tomorrow. Davie's coming to have a wee word with Nicola the day after a cross party committee at Holyrood took a long hard look at the Smith Commission proposals and said that they were in fact pretty rubbish to begin with, and have got increasingly rubbisher as Westminster gutted them. Despite the fact that the Smith Commission is losing credibility quicker than Jim Murphy is losing union support and Kezia Dugdale can say "SNP bad", in his mundellirium, our new Secretary of State for Unwanted Torydom still thinks that this is a final settlement for devolution. It's the charming naivety normally associated with a stuffed panda, so pretty much what we've come to expect from David Mundell then.

He pretty much alone in this opinion, just as he is alone in the opinion that his government can abolish the Human Rights Act and the Scottish Parliament will roll over and say, "Well that's OK then. Here's the other cheek of our arse, you can kick that too." Back in the real world it's hard to say what has a longer life expectancy, the Smith Commission proposals, Jim Murphy's career, or a scrofulous mayfly with dysentery.

It is thought that Nicola is going to present Davie with a shopping list of Scottish demands when he visits Embra the morra. How Davie responds will determine whether there will still be a United Kingdom in a few years' time. Some in his party are calling for him to make a definitive offer of full fiscal autonomy to kill off the demands for independence once and for all. But we've heard the one about killing Scottish nationalism stone dead before.

Wee Paddington Panda Mundell swore blind just a few days ago that the Smith Commission proposals were all that was on the table, so an increased offer from Cameron will just make him appear mundellirious and confused again, but that's par for the course with our new Secretary of State for Promotions Above His Paygrade. In the weeks and months to come he's going to become increasingly bemused.

## Resistance Is Fertile

*15 May 2015*

The Cameron one has deigned to bestow a visit upon the little Scottish people, who are decidedly unimpressed with his munificence. Caledonian ingrates. Davie promised, nay swore blind, that he'd look at proposals for further devolution. What more do those Pictish types want eh? David Cameron is actually going to think about Scottish devolution, and according to the fervid UK media, that's pretty much a guarantee that he's going to offer a new devolution settlement and kill Scottish nationalism stone dead again. In fact, it's cast iron and as solid as a vow from Gordie Broon, because that worked out so well for them the last time. Gordie promised all sorts of amazing super-powers, although the only one which materialised was the power of invisibility, and he kept that one for himself.

Mind you, a promise to look at something isn't quite the same as a promise to commit, get married, and settle down and get a Labrador puppy together. I might promise to go out on a hot date with a guy who gets fantastic write ups in the papers as god's gift to gorgeousness, but upon discovering he's Jim Murphy and the gorgeousness exists purely inside his own head then the date going to end at the soup course, with the soup over Jim's expansive head. In fact, that's pretty much what happened when Jim invited the voters of East Renfrewshire out on a five year engagement.

Despite the rejection, Jim's not taking no for an answer and is now stalking the Scottish body politic like a creepy ex-boyfriend with a wilted bunch of flowers he got from a BP garage in Neilston, begging us not to leave him and swearing blind that the next time he won't let us down. Although at least some of that Gordie Broon magic has rubbed off on him, and he's acquired the power of invisibility too.

The big difference between Jim and Davie is that there's no way that anyone, not even Alan Cochrane, can get away with claiming that Davie is approaching the topic with an open mind. Alan was on Sky News today complaining that the SNP had won too many seats, and causing his fictional memoirs to be remaindered in bookshops. Alan was convinced that he'd single-handedly defeated the forces of Alicsammin last year, and now those same forces are not only scoffing openly at his literary efforts, his beloved Union is at greater risk that it ever was and likely to end up unloved and unwanted in the bargain basement along with Alan's book.

To be fair, very few people in Scotland have an open mind where Davie is concerned, we've all seen how the Tories operate. We remember that in 1979 the Tories promised that if Scotland voted no to the limited home rule offer in that year's referendum that they'd give us something "better", and that something better turned out to be Maggie Thatcher. The trauma of that event caused a mutation in the Scottish genome leaving the Scottish electorate with a genetic immunity to the blandishments of the Conservatives. This means that the only person in the whole of Scotland who might qualify as open minded is the Secretary of State for Wibble, Fluffy Mundell, and his mind is only open because he's never learned how to do up the buttons at the back of his head.

So given this not insubstantial history of prior disappointments, the press headlines that the Tory government is open to considering the transfer of substantial new powers to Scotland are wishful thinking in much the same way that you can plant a feather and wish it would grow a chicken.

What's going to happen with Davie's promise is that Etonian eyes will glance upon the politely worded requests from north of the border, fulfilling Davie's media promise to look statesmanlike and like he gives a toss about Scotland, and then an Etonian gob will say "bugger off" in private, before making a public announcement to kick the entire topic into some committee of Andrew Dunlops from which it will never reappear. Expecting the Tories to come out with a substantive devolution offer is like expecting UKIP and the DUP to have a float at a gay pride march complete with a semi naked Nigel Farage and Ian Paisley Junior doing a pole dance. But that's just silly as Nigel wouldn't be seen dead dancing with an East European immigrant.

The Conservatives will never consent to substantial devolution for Scotland even though that's about the only thing that has half a chance of keeping the Union together. Davie Cameron is incapable of thinking beyond the next election, by which time it will be Boris Johnson's problem and Davie will care even less than he does at the moment. You wouldn't think that was actually possible, but it is. The Tories think of Scotland like a colonial possession, it's a place to go hunting shooting and fishing, which gives them somewhere to host their nuclear warhead small penis compensators and lets them indulge in the fantasy that British nationalism is a better kind of nationalism than any other nationalism because it's not a nationalism at all. That, and acting as a reservoir of natural resources and skilled labour, is Scotland's place in the Union. Our job is to make other people feel better about themselves.

But last year Scotland planted a seed of self-determination and discovered that resistance is fertile. Contrary to common belief, self-determination isn't solely about independence. It's about defining your own role and identity for yourself. Scotland hasn't voted for independence -yet - but that doesn't mean that we can't have self-determination within the United Kingdom for the time being. Scotland and the people of Scotland should be the ones to decide what role Scotland will play within the UK, not Davie Cameron, not the Tories, and not the Fluffellymundelly. Scotland will have greater powers sooner or later. No matter what delaying tactics Cameron employs he will not be able to withstand the tides that Scotland rides. His delays and obfuscation only make Scotland's demand and determination even stronger. Their resistance makes Scotland's determination more fertile and a thousand more wild bluebells flower independently.

And that's why we returned the Gael force of 56 SNP MPs to Westminster. The message they have for Westminster is that it is not up to Westminster to tell Scotland who or what Scotland is, Scotland will tell Westminster. They no longer define us.

They better listen.

# How to Kill a Coyote

*16 May 2015*

You can't kill the Coyote. Throw him off an electoral cliff so he plunges into a deep canyon which is impossible to climb out of, crush him under a boulder of votes, run him over with the on-coming Caledonian Express, he'll still pop up again in the next scene of the Labour cartoon, eternally dooming the party to comedy failure. Jim Murphy has crawled out from underneath another rock, saving his skin by just three votes in a confidence motion at Labour's Scottish HQ, but he has resigned anyway. Just not yet. In a wee while, next month. He has to hang around for a bit longer so that he can pretend he's got a shred of dignity left.

Jim won the vote of confidence by 17 votes to 14, which in a fundilymundelicious irony works out at 55% to 45%. But his three vote majority was not quite what it seemed. Jim voted for himself, he also secured the vote of a former member of M16 who now sits in the Lords and who was controversially drafted in at the last moment because Labour has only got one lonely MP left. The surprise nominee is a long standing ally of Jim's. After those two entirely predictable votes are discounted, really Jim won by just one vote, and that was Nicola Sturgeon's.

Jim did get the support of Ian Lonely Murray, Scotland's sole surviving Labour MP. But that was only because the Red Panda realised that as long as Jim stayed in post then he'd avoid most of the flak. Apart from him, Jim's political passing is mourned only by the plethora of parody accounts on Twitter, who will now turn their attentions to Ian.

So Jim had to go, but not just yet, because a succession of prominent figures in the Labour party south of the border had stated that the party was the party of working people, and the voters of East Renfrewshire sacked Jim from his job. According to the papers, Jim's resignation has thrown the party into turmoil, which does kind of make you wonder what it's been in up until now. Something that comes out of a bull's bum, I'm guessing.

Although I wasn't present at the meeting, I'd put money on Jim being told that he could have a nominal victory in his vote of confidence, but only on condition that he resigned. It's that manufactured dignity thing. It looks better in the papers, and allows both Jim and Labour to save a wee bit of face. Right up until Saturday morning Jim gave every indication that he was going to cling on to the post of leader like a dog turd on a leaky wellie without the slightest care that he was going to tread crap all over the party shag pile in the process. He was determined to remain leader even though he knew there was huge opposition against him. Jim showed no inclination to care that he was tearing apart the shattered remnants of the Labour party in Scotland. Yet by Saturday evening we were being informed that Jim didn't want to divide the party. Uh huh. That's so in character isn't it. I strongly suspect that Jim was given no choice - resign or the party would resign itself to giving him the boot.

In a bitter resignation speech, Jim blamed everyone but himself for Labour's woes. It was the fault of the SNP. It was the fault of the Tories. It was the fault of the voters for not listening to Jim. It was the fault of nationalisms everywhere, including in Tuvalu. It was the fault of previous Labour leaders for leaving abruptly. It was Johann Lamont's fault for not standing up to Jim constantly briefing against her. But mostly it was the fault of Len McCluskey and the unions for wanting Labour to be left wing.

Jim's not going to resign like previous Scottish leaders have resigned, before he goes he's going to work on a plan to reform the party. Mind you, Jim was the one who came up with the plan to reform the party after it was trounced in the 2011 Scottish elections, and that hasn't exactly worked out well for them. Mostly Jim's plan will be about getting one over Len McCluskey. Jim thinks it's wrong that Labour in Scotland can be dictated to by a guy sitting behind a desk in London, although he only objects when it's a trade union desk, not when it's the desk of a Labour front bench politician. Some London desks are more equal than others. So Jim's plan will be to take the last of labour out of Labour, and then hope and pray that Scotland's voters will vote for the nothing that is left.

Jim's not going to stand for Holyrood next year - "It's time for me to do something else," he said, like maybe finish his degree. But in the meantime he's off to enjoy a well-deserved break somewhere where there's far less infighting, strife and fundamentalist hatred than the civil wars which are consuming the Labour party in Scotland. Like Syria.

Jim's tenure as leader of Labour in Scotland ended the same way as it started, with Jim insisting that he knows better than everyone else. If the Labour hierarchy reward Jim's failure with a peerage, it will be their final death sentence and the party will never recover. Not that their prospects are looking great as it is.

So Jim's going to come up with a plan which he's expecting the new party leader to implement. At the same time however, this new leader, whoever he or she may be, will - according to Jim - have complete freedom to take the party in whatever direction they choose. Like for example choosing to take the party in a direction not determined by Jim and his hauf-airsed plans which were responsible for getting them into this mess in the first place.

It's not going to be easy to find a credible new leader, as Labour's gene pool is small and rapidly drying up. The choices are not inspiring, just when the party needs a leader with superhuman abilities. There's Kezia of course, and James Kelly - a man who makes Iain Gray seem warm and human. Whoever it is will not only have to repair Labour's tattered and threadbare rug, they'll also have to scrub out the crap trodden into it by Jim. And all this in time for the next Holyrood elections in May next year.

We're witnessing the end of days for Labour in Scotland. The party was founded as a tool of the labour movement, and it was killed by those who came to believe that the labour movement was just a tool of the Labour party. Not even Wile E Coyote himself could survive that one and live to run another day.

## Unleashing the Dogs of Woe

*18 May 2015*

I t says a lot about the priorities of our Tory overlords that one of the first votes in the Commons is to be a vote to legalise the barbaric cruelty of tearing apart creatures they don't control with creatures that they do control, taking blood stained pleasure from pain, and garlanding themselves in the entrails of entitlement. It's not just the intrinsic repulsion that anyone with a basic capacity for empathy feels towards the braying proponents of ritualised cruelty to animals, fox hunting is a metaphor for the Conservatives' view of the lower orders. Davie Cameron's government seeks to unleash the dogs of woe on all of us, and that has a lot to do with why fox hunting excites such strong passions. We are all foxes now.

Over the past few days there's been a lot of will they won't they about whether the SNP will oppose the Tories' attempts to reintroduce fox hunting in England. It's the classic example of an England only issue, and was even cited as such by Nicola Sturgeon during the election campaign when she was explaining why the SNP would vote against privatisation in the English NHS. Currently the SNP is the only party which is taking a party line on the issue of fox hunting. All the other parties treat it as a personal vote, and allow individual MPs to vote

143

according to the dictates of their own consciences. The SNP should do exactly the same.

A majority Tory government puts far bigger issues at stake than the rights of foxes, like for example the rights of human beings, the assault that is about to begin on the poor, the disabled, and the disadvantaged. But fox hunting is the traditional pursuit of the British upper classes and their implacable belief that they are born to rule, that they have the right to ride roughshod over anything and anyone which gets in their way. Fox hunting symbolises all of that, and that is what makes it such a powerfully emotive issue.

Standing up for foxes means standing up against the right of the Tories to ride roughshod over humans too. Good politics means recognising the power of symbolism. The SNP stands for an alternative to austerity, for opposition to Trident, for a new way of doing things. Opposing fox hunting is a symbol for that. It means standing up for the powerless against the powerful. Opposing fox hunting sends a message to the left in England that Scotland hasn't abandoned them, that we're not just looking out for ourselves. That we care. It's the symbolism of solidarity with a small ginger canine.

It doesn't matter that ripping apart foxes with the teeth and claws of dogs is a hoary old British tradition. It's torture, and torture is not culture. There are no great constitutional issues at stake here, although the Tories and their allies will try to pretend otherwise. What passes for a British constitution is a set of practices and precedent which the ruling classes make up as they go along in order to advantage themselves. Scotland's representatives in the House of Horrors should do exactly the same for Scotland's advantage. And defending the rights of foxes in England does bring advantage to Scotland - because it makes us friends and allies on the English left.

Nicola Sturgeon said during the election campaign that Scotland would work to bring progressive politics to the entire United Kingdom. This is a cost free way of achieving that, a small sign that Scotland will make its mark. We're all in this Union together, and it does Scotland no favours to be in a Union with a country whose legislators don't understand the difference between torture and culture. As long as we are in this Union, as long as Scots travel the world and are confused with "the English" because the rest of the world doesn't appreciate the difference between England and the UK, then Scotland has a moral duty to prevent the Conservatives from making England a laughing stock and an affrontment in the eyes of the world.

The SNP have yet to make a decision on how their 56 MPs will vote on the matter, but it won't be long before Cameron introduces his bill to prevent Scottish MPs from voting on English only issues. He's already announced his intentions to introduce legislation soon, so what does Scotland stand to lose by taking a moral stance on fox hunting while Scottish MPs still can? If the SNP abstains, the chances are that the barbaric practice will be legalised. However, if they vote against there are enough Tory rebels to give the foxes a running chance of escape.

If the SNP were to vote against the legalisation of tearing living feeling creatures limb from limb with a pack of dogs, Fleet Street would scream in unison that the party was interfering in English affairs, like it was a bad thing to be opposed bone crushing bloody pain and gratuitous cruelty to animals. Daily Mail editorial writers would have apoplexy, although to be honest that's normal for them, the Torygraph would thunder its disapproval, the Times would tut furiously, and the Guardian would be crushed between the weight of their last remaining liberal sentiments and their instinctive hatred for the SNP.

Scottish voters would look on the ensuing collective harrumphment of outraged outdated unionism and say, "Ha ha. Good!" Ensuring that fox hunting stays banned, upsetting the Tories, and pissing off the UK media all in one move, that's a result. That's a good day at the office that is. They have their blood sports, and we have ours. Ours are a lot more fun, and don't involve ripping living creatures apart - except metaphorically. Making the Tories angry and upset is, in part, what we elected all those SNP MPs for. The 56 are not there to make life easy for the defenders of barbaric traditions and the UK's OK yahs of privilege. So let's make things uncomfortable for them. I want to see Jacob Rees Mogg cry. Let's unleash the Scottish dogs of woe on him and the other upper class proponents of pain and privilege.

## Sitting Uncomfortably

*19 May 2015*

Are you sitting comfortably? This past week has given us a few significant news stories. There's the Royal Navy whistle-blower who has revealed that weapons designed to blow up half the planet and turn the other half into a radioactive wasteland are a disaster waiting to happen. In another example of rank insanity the Labour party in Scotland continues on its descent into self-obsessed madness, although it had snapped the elastic band of nutjobbery quite some time ago. Now it's twanging the ends on its forehead thinking that Ken Macintosh is the great new idea. Meanwhile the Tories are about to embark on an all-out assault on our civil and human rights, introduce a snoopers' charter and cut off the legs of the unemployed in order to teach them to stand on their own two feet. What passes for business as usual in this Great British northern province then.

So what's the big story that has got the metrocommentariat appalled and disgusted? Dennis Skinner had to get an SNP person to budge along a bench. It's an outrage. He's a pensioner. The SNP upset an old man. The basterts, setting their beach towels on House of Commons benches like German tourists. Uppity Scottish people demanding front row seats and wanting to be noticed. Where do they think they are? They should stand at the back of the chambers in reverent silence while the lizard aliens who are in charge make all the decisions. It's always worked like that before.

Mind you, if Davie Cameron really is a lizard alien you do have to wonder why he chose that face for his human form. He should have gone for something less shiny and smug and more believably human. Although to be fair, he was comparing himself to Boris Johnson and the dead fish eyes of George Osborne, and by those standards he's really done rather well.

But back to seating arrangements. Dennis Skinner is 83 and still sits as an MP. The only other people who continue in their jobs at that age are popes and African dictators. No one could ever accuse Labour MPs of infallibility, although many have accused them of kleptocracy - but never, it must be pointed out, Dennis Skinner. Dennis is a good man, but he's condemned himself to a fate worse than political death. He thought he was breaking the rules, but the establishment just rewrote the rules so that Dennis and his toothless yelled protests became a part of them.

A long time ago, back when there was still a Labour party in Scotland, Dennis used to be a real radical and a proper rebel with a yell. Then he became a Labour MP and over the course of the decades evolved into a tame pet of the British establishment. Dennis has taken upon himself the invaluable task of representing a peculiarly British safely contained and institutionalised awkwardsoddery. He has become the kind of revolutionary that revolves nothing except a children's roundabout of ritualised protest, it goes nowhere and serves only to amuse those who think they're the grown-ups.

Dennis sits on a front bench in the House of Commons and shouts out protests which allow the establishment to feel like they're really democrats and that freedom of speech is alive and well in the United Magic Kingdom of austerity. But everyone knows that Dennis has no sparkly wand and that nothing ever changes. That's how he can be described as a national treasure. He's become a faded red thread in the fabric of the cloth he once wanted to rip up. When a rebel has his own recognised place in the institution he's rebelling against he's no longer a rebel at all, he's just a species of court jester with worse jokes. He becomes the subject of the cruellest taunt you can make at an auld rebel: "The sowel, he means well."

It's because Dennis is a token rebel who changes nothing that he's now the darling of the British right wing press. When the Daily Mail is leaping to his defence you know he's no real threat to the established order but instead is a part of it. The British establishment is using Dennis as a stick to beat up on a group of MPs who really do threaten to change things. That's a bit of a come down - from the Beast of Bolsover to the neutered pet of the Tory press.

Dennis Skinner sits on his front seat bench as a warning to the 56 SNP MPs. Dennis in his special place railing against the institution that has institutionalised him should act as a permanent reminder of the fate the SNP's 56 need to avoid. They must not become co-opted and their protests ritualised and neutered. They must avoid becoming the tartan trimming in a Great British pageant. Westminster subverts those who seek to subvert it by demanding adherence to its rituals and its ancient traditions which were for the most part invented by Victorians in a fit of archaistic window dressing.

The SNP's MPs should sit wherever they damn well please, they should clap and cheer and have no regard for the childish and silly social rituals that underpin Westminster, because otherwise they become co-opted by them. They become Dennis Skinners, a part of an institution that isn't fit for government and a justification for things remaining as they are. They must never forget that they are not there to become a part of the Westminster furniture, they are there to act as a Scottish noise up in a cosy British establishment old boys club. They are they to annoy, to upset, to be a permanent thorn in the pink and flabby flesh of the lizard people.

But far more importantly Scotland's MPs must never allow the real issues to be swept under the Great British tapestry. Things which, it shouldn't need to be pointed out, are far more important than fox hunting or seating arrangements. They are there to shout and scream that the fabric is rotten and is woven out of the threat the Tories pose to our human rights, the demonisation of the poor, the axe that's being taken to the benefits of the vulnerable, the dangers of a nuclear missile programme mismanaged by muppets, the permausterity of government by the bankers for the bankers.

Scotland's MPs are there to resist and to point out that alternatives are possible. They are there to weave a new story. They are there to make sure that none of the representatives in that parliament are ever sitting comfortably.

# It's a Dog's Life

*20 May 2015*

According to Wednesday's Herald, a group of "experts" on devolution have said that there should not be another independence referendum for at least fifteen years. So that's us telt then, the experts say no. Mind you, at least one of the experts was a fully paid up member of the nawness faction during the referendum, so the fact he's saying no again counts as consistency, not as news per se. The reason that the period of fifteen years was chosen was because that's a generation as measured by teenage pregnancy, or the approximate life expectancy of a mongrel dug. It is immensely flattering that unionists think a wee ginger dug made such a contribution to the independence debate that they want to make sure he's popped his clogs by the time there's another. But this dug is going nowhere.

The whole generation thing originates in an off the cuff remark made by Alicsammin. Since the UK media and Unionist parties persuaded themselves that Scotland was really voting for Alicsammin in September 2014, they feel it's only right and proper that everyone else in Scotland ought to suffer from the same delusion. They fondly believe that the country rejected Alicsammin by 55% to 45% and so the Unionists are quite determined that Scotland shouldn't have a chance to vote for Alicsammin again until Alicsammin's ASBO has expired. However since the rest of us thought we were voting for or against independence, a large number of us don't feel bound by Alicsammin's conversational comments.

I certainly don't - no one asked me if I was agreeing not to want another independence referendum for a whole mongrel. I don't recall placing my X in a wee box marked YES in answer to the question: "If it's a No vote to Alicsammin do you agree to shut your gob and tug your forelock until your dog has died and then at such time as a Tory government deigns to allow Scotland to have another referendum because by participating in this referendum you are conceding any rights to an opinion?" I'm sure that wasn't the question.

The basic principle here is that it's not for Davie Cameron to be telling Scotland when we can have another referendum, we'll be telling him. That's what this democracy lark is all about after all. And let's not hear any of that guff about respecting the will of the 55%, because as I have previously argued - if there's going to be another referendum it will be because there is no longer a 55% whose will must be respected.

The truth is that while we may quibble with the experts' timing, we shouldn't have another independence referendum for a good while yet, for simple tactical reasons. If we have a referendum too soon, and without a material change in circumstances, the Yes side would lose, and that really would set back the cause of independence for a generation. A proper generation and not just a teenage pregnancy one like you get on all the poverty porn programmes on the telly. That said, Scotland should definitely have another independence referendum - but only when the Yes side knows we're going to win it. In the meantime, with a majority Tory government, we're in for a dog's life.

A week is famously a long time in politics. Fifteen years is an aeon. Fifteen years ago a modem was the height of internet speediness, we had animated gifs instead of video streaming, Facebook and Twitter hadn't been invented, and social media meant putting an advert in the classifieds in the Evening Times. There was no alternative media in Scotland and we relied almost entirely for our news on Reporting Scotland and the Daily Record. Not surprisingly Labour was utterly dominant, people didn't giggle every time a Liberal Democratic MSP was interviewed on telly, and idea of independence was the preserve of a marginalised SNP which was struggling to find a place for itself.

All sorts of things could change between now and 2030, none of which will be reported on Reporting Scotland if they're any good for Scottish independence. Although by then the Tories will have privatised the BBC and outsourced Scottish programming to Serco and we'll get getting wall to wall reality shows about poorly paid security guards in hi-viz jaikets chasing shoplifters, and an investigative programme in which the last person in the country who hasn't had their benefits sanctioned is hunted down with hounds - so pretty much like the telly is just now then.

If there's still a Reporting Scotland in 2030 you can be sure that it will still be doing a sterling service telling us about the important things that happen in Scotland, that would be the murrdurrs, the fitba, something about waiting times in hospitals and how it's all the fault of the SNP, wee cute kittens and mair fitba.

Back in the present day, the programme has just won an award for being the best Scottish news programme. No seriously. Reporting Scotland has won the RTS Scottish TV award ... Aye that's what I said too ... It's really the "Thank fuck Scotland voted No" award. And they wonder why the traditional media is rapidly losing credibility. Perhaps the RTS has a category for news programmes that try to present the Daily Record in video form, or the best presentation of Labour press releases. Or maybe it's because you can now get an award for finding new and inventive ways to say SNP bad. Someone ought to tell Kezia Dugdale.

A whole lot of things can change long before the fifteen years are up. There's the EU referendum looming, there's the impact on Scotland of five years of durrty Tory basterts. There's the still unanswered question of a devolution settlement. And there's a Scottish Parliament election in a year's time. Scotland can't tie its constitutional hands for an arbitrary period of time just to keep discredited politicians happy. It's not for them to be telling us, it's for us to be telling them. And we will tell them when we're good and ready for another independence referendum.

We'll be good and ready for one when Yes is certain to win it. It will be when Scotland is sick of the dog's life we live under the Tories and a British Labour party determined to ape them. We'll be good and ready for it when the 55% is no longer a 55%. That's not yet. But the clock is ticking on the dog's life.

## These Things Happen

*22 May 2015*

Not even Rona can help him now. The last shreds of Alistair Koalamichael's credibility have gone the way of Danny Alexander's career in politics, shot down in the flames of public disgrace. Although Danny Alexander did at least manage to salvage something that could pass - from a distance - as dignity. Alistair can't even do that, reduced as he is to writing apologetic letters to Nicola and the French ambassador begging for his career to continue.

The last Lib Dem standing, or at least crawling, has finally blubbered out what most of us had suspected, that he was responsible for leaking a memo which claimed Nicola Sturgeon wanted the Tories to win the General Election. The Dishonourable Member for Lying Gobshite only admitted it because he got caught, after an official investigation which cost the taxpayer almost £1.4 million - even though everyone knew all along that Alistair bears a startling resemblance to the creepy janitor in Scooby Doo, and it's always the creepy janitor who's the guilty party.

The thing about flinging crap is that it leaves you with shit on your own hands. The SNP have taken over from the Lib Dems as the third party, leaving the Lib Dems with just being the turd party. With the disappearance of his aiders and abetters with the near extinction of the Lib Dems and the Labour party in Scotland Alistair has now been left to juggle jobbies all by himself. Since he's clearly deficient in the crap coordination department, it is now raining down on his head, and on the heads of the media which gleefully reported the original smear. They'd hoped that they'd found the dam to stem the rising tide of the SNP, but they'd forgotten that you can't build a strong barrier on a foundation of shite. That's a lesson that Better Together would do well to remember after their campaign to save the Union.

In an attempt to make reparations, or at least buy himself some time in the hope that the problem will go away, Alistair has tendered a virtual resignation. The former Scottish Secretary has said that he'd have stood down from the job that he no longer has, the job he no longer has because his party was wiped out at the polls for telling lies. In other words, he has pretended to make amends in the hope that he'll be forgiven for real.

That's a bit like a bank robber offering to pay back some Monopoly money after spending the real ill-gotten gains on securing a nice wee pad in the Northern Isles. Naturally Alistair has no intention of giving up the cosy wee corner he's acquired for himself in the Northern Isles, the one he got on the back of claiming to the voters of Orkney and Shetland that unlike the rest of his lying party he wasn't a durrty lying bastert. Mind you, if he did announce that he was going to step down, no one would believe him.

Alistair has also said that he won't accept the severance pay he's due for losing his post as a Government minister, some £16000. He should be made to repay the entire cost of the investigation, although perhaps there needs to be an investigation into the investigation - and Alistair should pay for that too. Why did it take the best part of six weeks and around £1.4 million to discover that Alistair dunnit when his dirty crap smeared paw prints were all over the memo in the first place? When the investigation was announced he admitted that he knew who did it, so why did it take so long - and more importantly why were the findings of the investigation not released until the election was done and dusted?

The outcome of the investigation was clearly going to have a bearing on how people would have voted, and you can bet a stuffed koala that if it was likely that the investigation was going to discover that Nicola had indeed said what was alleged then the Lib Dems and Labour would have been screaming for it to conclude and publish long before May 7. But we all knew that it was going to finger a Lib Dem as a liar, and no one in power was about to do the SNP - or the voters of Scotland - any favours.

Mind you, they have previous for expecting Scottish voters to make their minds up on a prospectus that's a lie. This is why we've lost all faith in them, and is precisely why hundreds of thousands who've never voted SNP before voted SNP on May 7. A leopard can't change its spots, and a Unionist politician can't change their verbal diarrhoea. If you lie in court you can go to jail, if you lie to affect the outcome of an election you get a seat in the Commons and an expense account.

You can have a grudging respect for an underhand, ruthless, and Machiavellian self-serving manipulator. But not when they're also inept, transparent, and clueless. Alistair wanted to wield a stiletto, but he got mixed up between the wee Italian knife and the high heels. Unlike the guy in the Money Supermarket advert, who also has a well upholstered arse, Alistair teetered and fell off and twisted his ankle.

Now he's lying face flat on the floor, desperately hoping that he can get back on his feet before his arse is trodden into the shag pile of public disgrace. The weekend is dominated by calls for him to resign his seat amidst claims that he was elected on a false premise, that false premise being that he's not a lying manipulative underhand excuse for a balloon.

It's not clear if there is any mechanism by which Alistair can be held to account. Clearly he has no sense of shame, otherwise he'd never have embarked on a pathetically transparent smear campaign in the first place. It's possible that he may have broken electoral law - but if a politician could be held to account for not telling the truth we wouldn't have a Conservative party and Jim Murphy would never have existed.

There's now a petition demanding that Alistair stand down so there can by a by-election in Orkney and Shetland. 97% of those who have participated in online poll by the Shetland Times want him to go. Coincidentally, 3% was the size of his majority, so it now looks like only 800 voters in the Isles want him to remain as their MP. He might hang on to his job, but the 56 SNP MPs are going to make the next five years very uncomfortable for a man who may very well turn out to be the last Scottish Lib Dem MP ever.

These things happen, eh Alistair.

## The Dishonourable Dissembler for Porkies and Scrote-Lying

*23 May 2015*

The Dishonourable Dissembler for Porkies and Scrote-Lying is still occupying his ill-gotten seat, the one the representative for the Northern Isles got by misrepresenting himself to the Northern Islanders. Anyone with a shred of common decency would have resigned by now, but then anyone with a shred of common decency wouldn't have abused a government position and created a diplomatic incident in a crude attempt to smear an opposing party during an election campaign. So we should take it as a given that Alistair's title of "honourable" is meant ironically.

Apparently referring to a lying bastert as a lying bastert counts as unparliamentary language even when the lying bastert has admitted that he's a lying bastert. So any SNP MP who has to refer to Aliestair or address him in the Commons in future should call him their "Cough cough honourable um friend - oh are you still here then?" And learn how to pronounce honourable in quotation marks. But they should cut him out and refuse to acknowledge his presence unless it's absolutely necessary. He's there on false premises and he is illegitimate as an elected representative. People in Orkney and Shetland didn't know they were voting for a liar.

The Dishonourable Dissembler isn't being faced with a barrage of calls for his resignation from certain persons who seemingly make a weekly call for someone to resign. Which is odd. The leader of the Lib Dem groupuscule Wullie Rennie doesn't feel he's done a week's work unless he's called for the head of someone or other, preferably during an interview on BBC Scotland. It's the only way he can reassure himself that he's still alive and still has some sort of purpose, just imagine how depressing and pointless it would be to be a Lib Dem politician otherwise. It's as null pointery as a UK Eurovision entry, but without the self-knowing campery or the sparkly frocks. Mind you, Tavish Scott did once grow a beard, but no one was ever going to mistake him for Conchita Wurst.

Over the course of this Scottish Parliament, Wullie Rennie has called for the resignations of Alicsammin for being the head honcho of SNP badness, Justice Minister Kenny Macaskill also for assorted SNP badness, head of the Scottish Council for Voluntary Organisations Martin Sime for being - according to Wullie - too indulgent of SNP badness, and Chief of Police Scotland Stephen House for stopping and searching people who might not have been SNP supporters. He's called on several other individuals to resign too, generally for SNP badness. You can probably spot the theme.

The only person Wullie hasn't called on to resign so far is a man who has actually admitted to lying, admitted to abusing public office, and admitted to attempting to cover it all up so he could deceive the electorate. It's entirely coincidental that that man is also a Lib Dem isn't it. On Wullie Rennie's bus if it's not SNP badness it's not sufficiently bad for him to tell you to get off.

But Wullie is keeping very quiet in case people ask him precisely what he knew about the leak and when he knew it. The chances that he didn't know it originated from the office of the blubbering Scottish Secretary are about the same as the chances of the Lib Dems being wiped out if there's a by-election in Orkney and Shetland. It would be interesting to know what senior Labour figures knew about the origin of the smear too, seeing as how they were suspiciously well prepared when the story first broke. But then they all lost their seats in the election, so no one cares any more. It's just one more duplicity to add to the ones they've already been punished for. Aliestair however, is still clinging on. Maybe BBC Scotland will hound him until he resigns eh?

BBC Scotland is quite keen on calling for resignations too. The BBC hounded the former transport minister Stewart Stevenson to resign for SNP badness, too much SNP snow, and looking like a separatist version of Father Jack. But they don't seem hugely bothered by the Koalamichael. The difference is that even though Stewart Stevenson wasn't directly responsible for the snow it was SNP snow, whereas although Aliestair called up the blizzard of lies and deceit surrounding him all by himself it's not SNP snow. In the Pacific Quay news management department that's quite effective at clearing things up and they can ignore the heatwave of public protest that's melting Aliestair's career.

The snow storm clouds are gathering, despite the best efforts of the Lib Dems to hide under a snow blanket and make like they're purer than the driven snow. According to the Guardian, the Parliamentary Commissioner for Standards is set to investigate. Apparently they do have standards at Westminster, news which comes as a great surprise to most of us. Clearly they are not very high standards, but even with the bar set so low that it exonerates the expenses fiddlers of the Commons, the Dishonourable Dissembler is unable to clear it.

The new rules against lying to voters, introduced during the last Parliament at the insistence of Nick Clegg - now there's irony - state that if an MP is suspended from the House of Commons for longer than ten days then the electorate in his or her constituency can force a by-election. All it requires is for 10% of voters in the constituency to sign a petition to that effect and the MP in question can face the judgement of the voters even if he or she declines to do the honourable thing. So get collecting those signatures, Orkney and Shetland people.

The gravity of the offence committed by Aliestair is such that it's considered highly likely that he would be suspended from the House for longer than ten days. If that happens, his career is as good as over. He won't be missed.

But let's give the last word to the Dishonourable Dissembler himself. In an article penned for the Shetland Times after Labour MP Phil Woolas was stripped of his victory and the courts ruled that there had to be a by-election because Woolas had smeared his opponents, the Koalamichael wrote:

*"The right to freedom of speech is a fundamental one but it does bring a responsibility with it to tell the truth. The right to smear an opponent is not one we should be defending."*

Quite.

## Westminsteritis and Hyperkenezia

*25 May 2015*

The dishonourable Aliestair Koala has told the BBC that he's got no intention of resigning his seat and allowing voters in Orkney and Shetland the chance to decide whether they want a liar and smear-merchant to represent them in the House of Commons. He thinks he should be judged on how he's been as a constituency MP for the past 14 years and not his actual sins, which is a bit like a 1970s BBC radio DJ telling the judge to sentence him based on his work for charidee. How dare people want to judge him for his duplicity and underhand dealings. Aliestair doesn't seem to realise that he doesn't get to be his own judge and jury. He's suffering from Westminsteritis. The only cure is to separate him from his privilege.

But then Aliestair doesn't believe he's really told a lie at all. When he told reporters that the first he knew about the memo was when a reporter asked him about it, what he really meant was that it was the first time he'd read the entire text in full. Which is like claiming you have no part in a robbery because you only planned it and drove the getaway car but didn't set foot in the bank vault. Sadly for the Lib Dems and their Labour fences, Aliestair drove the getaway memo off a cliff, more the Italian Job than the French one. He only told them to blow the bloody diplomatic corps off.

However this raises more questions than it settles. Does Aliestair really think it's a defence to claim that he authorised the leak of something which he hadn't read? Is he trying to claim that he leaks things without knowing their content? The last time anyone leaked so indiscriminately they were immediately referred by their GP to the continence clinic.

It's not exactly a surprise that the last Lib Dem crawling has acquired a moral compass as mythical as the compassionate conservatism that was supposed to be a hallmark of the coalition that killed the party. Wee Wullie Rennie, who has made a career out of calling for people to resign, still can't understand what all the fuss is about. That's not really a surprise either. This is not unrelated to the fact that Wullie is so slow on the uptake that it will be the end of July before he realises that there's been a General Election. Wullie still can't understand why no one gets on his bus anymore.

Wullie is aided in his amnesia by much of the Scottish media, which is currently in full on move along now nothing to see here mode. They don't want to talk about Aliestair anymore. Aliestair is boring, he's dull, although of course we already knew that anyway. He's yesterday's story, the fish wrapper of politics and only those with chips on their shoulders still throw salt in the Lib Dems' wounds. Let's move on, there must be an SNP bad story along any minute now. Business as usual in North Britain.

Compare and contrast with how our supposedly free and fair Scottish media would be screaming if it was an SNP politician who'd been caught smearing in the same way. Glenn Campbell, who went to the same school as Aliestair, would be off in France filming a special programme for BBC Scotland, door-stopping random French people to ask them whether Scotland's reputation had been damaged *grossemente, beaucoup,* or *totalemente.* He'd currently be in a bistro in Marseilles greeting into a croissant about how Aliestair had made us all ashamed to be *ecossais.*

Neil Hay, the unsuccessful SNP candidate for Edinburgh South, was subject to more condemnatory column inches and airtime aspersions for tweeting a link to a BBC Scotlandshire article, which the media spun into a full on attack on the entire No voting public. Which only goes to prove that the Scottish media is itself an enthusiastic participant in smearing and therefore scarcely has the moral right to call on a politician to resign for behaving like a newspaper.

Meanwhile, there's also an attempt to go back to North British business as usual over at the Labour party in Scotland. Ken Macintosh has claimed that the party machine is bullying his supporters in order to sew the leadership election up for Kezia Dugdale. Does Labour have a machine left? It was last seen lying rusted and broken in a field in East Renfrew, where it has been used, none too successfully, in order to harvest Conservative votes for Jim Murphy. Accusations of bullying and intimidation are par for the course with the dysfunctional Labour party in Scotland, the difference between the

Labour party in Scotland and a cybernat is that Labour do it professionally.

It probably makes no difference whether Ken wins or Kezia wins, they're both most noted for their insistence that it's all the fault of the SNP. Ken is an ally of Jim Murphy, and Kezia was Jim's deputy. It's tweedlemurphken and tweedlemurphkeez. They could save everyone a lot of bother by standing as a joint candidate and make like a celebrity couple and call themselves Kenezia. Then the Scottish media can hype them up like they always hype a new Labour leader and we can have hyperkenezia, which sounds very like a medical condition involving uncontrolled tics and spasms and a slow and lingering demise. So it's really quite appropriate for the Labour party in Scotland then.

Some want Labour in Scotland to split from the British party and set itself up as a new autonomous party, possibly to be called the Pity Party. Then they could invite Aliestair Koalamichael to join. He's the only other person in Scotland who's in as much denial as Labour is.

It's only a couple of weeks since the election but they've already proven that when it comes to feeling sorry for themselves, Aliestair and Labour's surviving politicians are even more expert than all those other Lib Dem and Labour MPs who actually lost their seats. It looks like they are all suffering from hyperkenezia and their condition is terminal.

## Malkied by Malkie and Primed by Primula

### 26 May 2015

Aliestair's still there, clinging onto the face of Scottish politics like a particularly obstinate plook despite the increasingly intense squeezing of ordinary Scottish punters who are not enamoured that one of our elected representatives got his comfy well-padded seat into a comfy and well-padded seat on the basis of lies and smears. In Scotland the conduct of the Unionist parties, their sense of entitlement, their arrogance, their self-interestedness, was the real issue of the recent General Election, and Scotland squeezed them out of office and wiped its face with the Clearasil of electoral oblivion. One spot was out of reach, and it was only after the election that we discovered just how pustuliferous it is.

The urge to squeeze it is overwhelming, and we're not resisting the urge. Scotland's voters set out to clean up Scotland's politics, only now we discover that a nasty smell remains because it was disguising itself behind a delayed release air freshener. One of those expensive ones it bought with our money.

But opening the windows to clear out the smell is a witch hunt, because it's the punters who are doing the pursuing, and that makes it borderline fascist and the

171

harbinger of a one party state. However when pretty much the entire UK media hound an SNP politician, it's investigative journalism and evidence of the robust good health of British democracy. Just so we're clear on the hierarchy of hounding, they're a press pack, we're the hounds of hell and the curse of the curs. We're the self-righteous priggish pugs of Michael White's disapproving tuts.

The story refuses to die, despite the news breaking on a Friday before a bank holiday when it was hoped that attentions would be diverted by diversions, despite the disapproval of the Guardian's Michael White. It was kept alive over the holidays by social media, up against the rapidly waning interest of most of the traditional media. It was only a little lie, not a big lie. A little lie is of no concern to the big men, little lies only bother little people. How dare we be bothered, we should look at their faces. Are they bovvered? They're not bovvered.

The on Tuesday the Lib Dem's Malcolm Bruce attempted to put the story to rest by ramming a rocket up its arse and sprinkling it with the sparkly dust of incomprehension. We should forgive and forget because all politicians tell lies, said Malcolm, smoothing down the ruffled feathers of public trust by walloping them with a ball pin hammer and rubbing them with sandpaper. Why, he said like it was a bad thing, if we got rid of every politician who had told a lie then there would be no one left in Westminster. You don't say, said the public, as it gazed upon the Westminster seats that were once occupied by Danny Alexander, Magrit Curran and Jim Murphy.

And now, Malkie harrumphed, the SNP are trying to bully poor Aliestair out of office, because the poor wee lambie abused his position of power to act like a bully. It's just so terribly unfair. How dare ordinary people express an opinion. How dare they say they don't want to be represented by a liar and a smear merchant. The next thing you know they'll be demanding that their MPs are accountable - and where would we be then. We'd be living in a democracy, perhaps.

It has seemingly passed Malkie by that the reason we malkied his colleagues in the recent General Election was because we had discovered that they'd been telling us lies, and we're fed up with it. Lib Dems more than any party ought to realise the electoral consequences of telling lies to the electorate. It's a lesson that's flown over the top of Malkie's head. He can't even blame the ruinous cost of student fees for his inability to grasp the lesson, even though it's one we've given his party for free.

Malkie's maulications have reignited the story. Aliestair must be grateful that he's got such helpful friends. But then, coming over the hill like the Seventh Cavalry comes Michael White of the Guardian, bewailing the prigs of the SNP. Not being a middle class southern English person, I've never been entirely sure what a prig is, so it's a strange insult to hurl at working class Scottish people. The first rule of invective is to make sure that your barbs are felt by their recipients and they are duly wounded by them. I always thought a prig was someone who was excessively prim and proper, clearly not. But then

Michael is only a little prim, he's Primula - because he's White, cheesy, and smeary.

In a jaw-dropping opinion piece, the supposed bastion of liberal Britain allowed Primula to defend the right of politicians to lie to the public. From his lofty position floating above the little people in his Westminster bubble, Primula know that we're all Lt Kaffees in Westminster world, we can't handle the truth.

In Primula's universe it's more important to protect the lying Lib Dems from the electorate than it is to protect the electorate from lying Lib Dems. The only people who should judge Aliestair should be the people of Orkney and Shetland, said Primula primly, but without allowing them any mechanism for doing so.

Out in the real world in the Northern Isles, a campaign is underway to raise funds to start a court case to force a by-election. So that the people of Orkney and Shetland can judge Aliestair for themselves. If you haven't donated yet, it's well worth giving a quid or two.

But mainly Primula defends the lie because the lie is better than the alternative - at least when the alternative is the SNP. Aliestair must be allowed to remain as a point of principle, and that principle is SNP bad, SNP very very bad. Bad SNP bad. Primula knows that the SNP is bad because everyone who is anyone in the Westminster bubble says so. Westminster's definitions are the only definitions allowed. We're not allowed to think for ourselves, we're not allowed to define ourselves. And we're certainly not allowed to hold liars and dissemblers to account.

Aliestair must be crapping himself as he wonders who is going to stand up for him next.

## A Parp in a Bin and Clapping Chagrin

*28 May 2015*

Fluffy Mundell, the original Scottish political panda, was proving as evasive as the fluffy black and white variety on Wednesday as he avoided giving a straight answer to a simple question. His attempts to avoid the question were clear to anyone who listened, because Fluffy is not exactly as sharp as a pin, he's more a parp in a bin. Paddington Mundell thinks sleight of hand means waving a roof tile, so he's having very little success in deflecting awkward questions about his role in the infamous memo leak. He's standing on the roof and looking like a target.

So far Fluffy has managed to avoid questions by being invisible, but he couldn't avoid the cameras on the day of the Queens Speech, what with him being the only government MP in all of Scotland. It's a lonely job at the Scotland Office when all he's got are his teddy bears for company. Asked whether he knew anything about the infamous memo leaking, Bumfluffy replied that the enquiry said it was all down to Aliestair. He didn't say "No, I knew nothing about it", which is what you might expect a person who knew nothing about it to say.

Ali and Fluff have been playing Scotland Office tag team for the past five years, and it's not like it's an enormous office with thousands of staff and a hugely demanding work load. By all accounts the pair sat opposite one another in the same office. What Ali knew, Fluffy would have known too - unless he was taking the bin out at the time. But Fluffy stuck to his repetitious line that the enquiry had only found Aliestair to be at fault, which was a bit like Ronnie Kray saying that the courts had only found Reggie guilty. Fluffy shifted uncomfortably and the Scotland Office bin lid visibly lifted as the faint whiff off lie-fart was released.

Scotland is famously or infamously the land where I kent his faither, the traditional way of saying that in Scotland we don't have six degrees of separation, it's more like one or two. I don't ken Aliestair Carmichael's faither, but I know someone who did, someone who has known Aliestair since he was a wee stuffed teddy. This friend says that they were shocked by the leak and smear and Aliestair's role in it, because it's so out of character for him. I believe my friend.

My friend also said that they couldn't understand why Aliestair had done it, since he didn't stand to gain personally from it. And this is true - out of all the Lib Dem MPs in the UK, it was widely believed by one and all that if the Lib Dems would cling on anywhere, it would be in Orkney and Shetland. Despite an SNP tsunami that was even greater than the SNP had hoped or the Lib Dems and Labour had feared, Aliestair did indeed cling on to his seat. He could have avoided any smearing and underhand behaviour, and he'd currently be a respected figure, the noble survivor like the last of the Mohicans.

Instead he's hounded and hiding and his career may not survive.

So why did he do it? Did someone put him up to it, and what was he promised for doing it? Did he really put his career on the line in order to save Danny Alexander and Jo Swinson's skin without there being anything in it for him? The enquiry restricted itself to identifying the source of the leak, and our mainstream media shows no great appetite for getting to the bottom of these questions so it's unlikely we will ever know. We only know that the guy who looks like the creepy janitor did it, but we'll never know who put him up to it. It's not a very satisfying conclusion to a cartoon, even if we do manage to get him to stand down. Where's Scooby Doo and Mystery Inc. when you need them?

The UK media is occupied with far weightier issues than trying to find out who tried to pauchle a democratic election and piss off the French. The SNP clapped in the House of Commons, and the massed ranks of Daily Mailesque commentaries are showing their chagrin. Clapping is unparliamentary behaviour and only goes to show that Scottish people can't be trusted off a Unionist leash. Next thing you know they'll be being stereotypical on Dennis Skinner's bench. You can lie, you can smear, you can abuse public office for party gain, you can cause a diplomatic incident, you can pauchle your expenses, you can cover up the activities of well-connected paedophiles, you can cheat, you can start an illegal war that causes the deaths of hundreds of thousands. Just don't clap, because that's beyond the pale.

In the House of Commons the approved means of showing approval is to bray like a public schooldonkey by uttering a strangulated heeyah heeyah. The House of Commons likes strangulated because that's how they treat dissent. But there are no laws which say that upon being elected to the House of Commons you have to forget the social norms of the people who elected you and start acting like you're a privately educated person from Rightupyerainarseshire. It's merely a social convention, and the really interesting thing about a social convention is that if you break it often enough and persistently enough, then the social convention gets quietly rewritten.

So the SNP should continue to clap when they want to show approval. They should continue to act like normal people, like the people who elected them. Then they will rewrite the social conventions of Westminster so that they represent the people who put those MPs there instead of those MPs becoming bent out of shape by the norms of Westminster. I want an MP who will force Westminster to be representative of the people, not an MP who becomes representative of Westminster. I want an MP who knows that it's OK to clap, it's not OK to lie, cheat, smear, pauchle expenses or start illegal wars.

I know which is more offensive, and it sure as hell isn't clapping.

## Apres Moi Lied the Stooge

*29 May 2015*

He's still there. Aliestair Koalamichael hasn't resigned and shows no inclination to accept the proper consequences for his wrong doings. He's doing his damnedest to keep out of the public eye, with the exception of a tweet saying that it will all blow over. He's going to keep out of the public's way until it does. He'll be a very long time hiding then. It won't blow over for Aliestair and it doesn't matter how long he tries to hide. The smearer has smeared himself, he's stained his reputation indelibly. This is all he's ever going to be remembered for, the only notable event in his undistinguished career.

Today Orkney and Shetland residents lodged legal papers at the Court of Session challenging his election, having received sufficient funds from public donations to enable them to start legal action. The fundraiser is still short of the total required however, so keeping donating.

Taking legal action is the only way that the people of Orkney and Shetland can get their say. For all the cant in the media and from politicians that the only opinions which are important are those of Aliestair's constituents, the only way they can express their opinion is via the ballot box at a by-election. It's Aliestair who is denying them the chance to do that. He says he wants to be judged on his record as a constituency MP, but it's not up to him to decide what he gets judged on. That's for the electorate of Orkney and Shetland.

But Aliestair doesn't want them to judge him at all, he just wants to accept the power and the pay packet, he doesn't want to pay the moral bill. He wants to sit as a legislator and tell the rest of us what the rules are, and what the consequences for breaking those rules will be - but he himself thinks he should be beyond them. That's why his electorate have started their fundraiser, and that's why today they're lodging a case at the Court of Session.

The case may not succeed. The law is stacked in favour of the legislators. But even if Aliestair does survive the legal action, it still won't blow over for him. From now until the day he dies, Aliestair will be the smeary lie guy. That's what he'll be known for, and what his obituary will say. In years from now when academics discuss the death of the Liberal Democrats and Aliestair's role in it, his smear, the lie, and Aliestair's refusal to accept that he should have to pay the price is all that will be mentioned.

His legacy is a lie and his reputation is a smear. He's the Septic Bladder of Orkney. He'll be the man who took the power but not the responsibility, which is the prerogative of the harlot through the ages. He's the chancer who took the benefits but who refused to accept the cost. He's the smug arrogant face of the ancien regime whose defenders claim that he should be allowed to remain in post as he's all that stands between Scotland becoming a one party state - apres moi, lied the stooge.

Aliestair may yet survive, but this will never blow over for him. He has now attained the quite remarkable status of being the only politician the public take less seriously than Wullie Rennie. Everything he says in future, every public statement, every opinion piece, every intervention in a Parliamentary debate or contribution to a committee meeting, will be heard through the amplifier of his hypocrisy and deceit. All that will be heard is - "I'm a liar and a smearer." The people of Orkney and Shetland are now effectively without a representative, as their representative only represents the reprehensible. Every time he makes a speech, every time he tries to make a point, it can be countered with one simple statement - "But Alistair, you've already admitted that you're a liar." No one need ever believe anything that he ever says again. The Northern Isles deserve better than that.

Because of Aliestair's refusal to accept the consequences, he's tainted what is left of his party and signed death warrant for the shattered remnants of what was once a proud Scottish political tradition. The Lib Dems are in an even worse shape than the Labour party, and things are pretty desperate when you realise that you are an object of Kezia Dugdale's pity.

The party hasn't helped itself with its attempts to defend him. Malcolm Bruce's defence is that everyone lies so it's fine for us to lie too. What they don't seem to have realised is that it's because they all think it's fine to lie that we voted them out of office in May's General Election. And since they've not learned yet, then there will be a further price to pay. Tavish Scott seems to have grasped that point now, with his attempts to distance himself from Aliestair by telling us how angry and upset he is. But not angry and upset enough to call on Aliestair to resign.

Tavish Scott may lose his seat in Shetland in next year's Scottish elections, and wossisface might lose in Orkney - the MSP who is the nonentity's nonentity. There are submarine trenches with a higher profile than Liam McArthur. Tavish tells us that Aliestair told him on the Sunday following the election that he'd been responsible for the leak. Tavish didn't think to tell the rest of us or to tell the official investigation. Why did it take so long for the investigation to release its findings anyway?

Despite the British state, the Lib Dems, and much of the UK media rushing to his aid, Aliestair's career is as good as dead. It's not so much that they want to protect him as an individual, but the possible loss of Orkney and Shetland to an SNP MP deals a devastating blow to one of the Unionists' favourite arguments against Scottish independence - the claim that Orkney and Shetland would prefer the tender mercies of Westminster and would reject Scotland. There has never been any evidence to support this claim, and should the islanders ever elect an SNP MP the scare would finally die an overdue death.

But in rushing to defend Aliestair they only make it more likely that the pissed off voters of the Northern Isles would return an SNP representative at the Holyrood elections next year, and in terms of destroying Westminster's claim that the Northern Isles would secede from Scotland, that would be far more significant than a Westminster by-election in the islands. As has been constantly repeated by the SNP, the General Election was not about independence and did not provide a mandate for independence. That might not be the case with the next Scottish elections.

Public anger at the Lib Dems is growing with every day that Aliestair remains, and that makes it increasingly likely that the Northern Isles will vote for an SNP representative who is standing on a mandate for an independence referendum.

## Internalised Scottophobia and Self-Inflicted Rhinectomies

*31 May 2015*

The Labour party has expelled a member in Glasgow because he said on social media that he intended to vote SNP at the election. That's fair enough you might think, when you join a political party you should support that party and not tell folk you're going to vote for someone else. Otherwise it would be like working for a sweetie shop and telling potential customers that soor plooms are really bad for their teeth and their health and they ought to munch on some healthy alternatives instead. In fact, it's exactly like that, as it is also true that voting for Labour's Scottish soor plooms makes us toothless, and in excess can lead to a political diabetic coma. So it really is just as well that Scotland opted for the politically healthy alternative.

Anyway, this isn't going to be one of those hand wringing articles about what Labour needs to do in order to win back voters. Although we've really not had enough of those had we? No, this is just a blog for pointing and mocking, because I'm one of those nasty and divisive nationalists that Daily Mail journalist Chris Deerin greets about in his offensively nasty and divisive articles. Deerin and his pals in the cosy wee testosterone driven clique of the Scottish media pack are now greeting that another journalist, Derek Bateman, has broken the omerta and has called him out for it. Apparently it's wrong to criticise what a journalist writes, even when that journalist writes keech.

I've gone way past wanting Labour to get its act together, now I just want it gone for good, which in Deerin's world probably makes me an enemy of freedom of speech. But then I understand that while freedom of speech gives a journalist the right to say offensive things, I also understand that it also gives everyone else the right to tell that journalist that they're being a dickhead.

Chris Deerin writes articles that no English journalist could write because they would - rightly - be accused of racism, but just because you're Scottish it doesn't give you a free pass and automatic immunity from spouting anti-Scottish racism. It just makes you an Uncle Tam. Some of the most offensive homophobia has originated from the mouths and pens of people who are themselves gay - it's called internalised homophobia. When you live in a society which denigrates and demeans gay people, you can take on those attitudes yourself. Social norms are contagious.

Clearly you can get internalised Scottophobia as well, and it manifests itself in abundance in the tortured scribblings of the Unionist Scots of the UK media, living and working as they do in an environment whose social norms require that Scotland and its inhabitants are regularly demeaned and denigrated. They should be more objects of scorn and pity than of anger.

But back to Labour's dickheads and the institutionalised self-harm that passes for internal Labour party politics. Apparently without any attempt to allow the expelled party member to have a say, a letter was sent to an individual in Glasgow South telling him he was out of the party because he'd stated on social media that he was going to vote for "the Scottish Nationalist Party". The letter came from Labour's "compliance officer" in Newcastle, who was clearly unaware that the name is Scottish National Party. And there was us thinking that Scottish Labour was totally autonomous and self-governing. Is that not what Jim Murphy assured us during the election campaign? But now we find out that members are expelled on the say-so of a compliance officer in UK Labour - and without any opportunity to defend themselves.

It's certainly the case that party members shouldn't be advocating support for other parties during an election campaign. The SNP wouldn't look kindly upon a party member who was telling people to vote Labour instead of SNP. But there's a big but, a butt that's bigger even than some of the Scottophobic airses who write for the Daily Mail or the Telegraph. During the election campaign there were prominent Labour members who were urging people to vote for the Lib Dems or even the Tories in order to keep out the SNP. There was even a wee group of Labour canvassers in Perth who were assisting the local Conservatives. There were Labour candidates in these seats. Have those Labour people received letters from the compliance officer too? You can put money on the likelihood that they won't have.

It's only SNPBad that is capable of provoking Labour's knee jerk condemnation.

You'd think that a party that was losing its life blood more quickly than an extra in a Hammer Horror movie would look for a Dr Van Helsing instead of lying in a pity bath and slashing its arteries. Just how many members does Labour have left in Scotland? It's not like they can afford to expel the few they have left. After the leadership election which lumbered us all with Jim Murphy, the party refused to release the actual number of members who had participated in the vote - and our supine and spineless media refused to pursue them on the matter. That would be those journalists who are immune from criticism. Instead they accepted at face value Jim Murphy's insistence that the party has "around 20,000" members. And they had straight faces at the time.

Just a few days after Labour's catastrophic performance in the General Election, Ian Bayonetting the Wounded Davidson stated in an article in the Scotsman that many Labour members in Scotland were not really members at all, and added that the real membership figures were "so low as to be embarrassing". So it's obvious that Labour needs to be engaging with its diminishing membership and discovering why they're not inclined to vote for the party. Instead it just wants to indulge in a bout of self-inflicted rhinectomy to teach its face a lesson.

Meanwhile the Scottish media, if it wants to retain any credibility at all, must press the party to reveal its real membership statistics when it announces the result of its next leadership contest. But that's about as likely to happen as Labour getting over its knee jerk SNPBadness and embarking on a collaborative and constructive opposition to the real threat - a Conservative government. Scotland has chosen the SNP to oppose the Tories, and now we're choosing to build a new media as well.

## An Email from a Homophobic Bigot

*1 June 2015*

So here we are, slapping ourselves on the back about how Ireland has joined Scotland, England, and Wales in legalising gay marriage. Look at us, telling ourselves that we're all so progressive and forward looking. But LGBTI people still have to face many challenges and many hurdles. Homophobia is still a big problem. Bigotry is still putting shackles on personal self-determination, it's still a nasty illness of the body politic. Homophobia is a hatred that remains a stain on our society. It hasn't gone away. It still blights lives.

A couple of weeks ago I was contacted by someone (whose anonymity I will protect) asking me for advice about coming out as gay to his Catholic family. He was worried that his parents and his brother would reject him. He reads this blog and I am the only openly gay person he felt able to contact. It was an honour and a privilege to be approached by him for advice even though I am no therapist or counsellor, and I worry that my advice to him may not have been the best. His story illustrates that sadly homophobia is still an issue in this country. It's still an issue for the independence movement.

Homophobia is not a specifically Catholic issue, or even a religious one. Bigots will always find some justification for their fear and hatred. We may have legal gay marriage, homophobia may be defined as a hate crime, but there is no room for complacency. There are no laurels to rest upon.

The only way we can achieve true equality for all is to remain eternally vigilant, to challenge homophobia whenever or wherever it occurs. But the victims of homophobia are precisely those who are unable to challenge it, who lack the resources to speak out, who suffer the consequences of the narrow mindedness of others. That makes it all the more vital that those of us who can speak out do so.

All I can do is speak of my own experience. Here is the reply I sent to the request for advice.

*My own parents are pretty devout Mass going Catholics too, I came out to them way back in the late 1980s, and they didn't take it well. My dad didn't speak to me for seven years. My mum went through a long period of denial - claiming on the one hand that she accepted it and had no problem with it but on the other she didn't want to know anything about anyone I got involved with - and claiming it was me who had the problem not her. That went on for a couple of years.*

*It's all water under the bridge now. But it took a long time. They didn't really learn to accept the fact I am gay until I had been living with my late partner for a couple of years and they realised that I was happy and contented and holding down a well-paying job. My dad only really came round several years after that when I donated sperm for lesbian friends and he realised that unless he got it together he was never going to have a relationship with his granddaughters.*

*There's no easy answer or solution here. Partly it depends on how old you are and what your circumstances are - do you still live at home with your parents or have you long since moved out and grown up? If you're young and still living at home it might be better not to tell them until you've got your own place and are no longer dependent on them financially or otherwise. If you are a teenager then you might have to deal with them being convinced it's a phase that you're going through - which is a form of denial on their part.*

*If you're older it's easier in the sense that you're not risking losing the roof over your head if it all goes wrong - and even if it goes well there's going to be an uncomfortable period of adjustment. Even then you might not want to tell them until such time as you're involved in a serious relationship. That's why I finally told my parents - after I met Andy.*

*Do you have adult siblings? It might be easier to tell a sister (who are generally more sympathetic than brothers) first and elicit her support before tackling your parents. Alternatively, it might help to speak to a supportive aunt or uncle first. Ask them to be with you when you tell your parents. It can help to defuse the situation.*

*However - whatever age you are you need to ensure that you have a good network of supportive friends/relatives before telling people who are important to you, but whom you know are not going to take the news well. That way when or if you do tell your parents, you won't feel alone and isolated.*

*Anyway, I hope things work out for you.*

I got a short reply saying that he was going to sound out his friends and family for people who wouldn't have a problem with him being gay. He said my advice was helpful, and I was glad that in some small way I might have helped.

And that was that, until Sunday evening. I received the following message from the same email account. I've copied it verbatim, spelling mistakes and all.

*I was gonna post this on youre shitey blog so the world could know what you did to my brother but I don't wanna give a fag like you my email address so you can creep on me. Luckily [name removed] is too stupid to close his emails.*

*I just want to tell you that, like all homos who pretend to support independence you need to take a long, hard look at yourself. Your way of life is one that was brought into our country by the paedos at Watemonster, and protected by Tories and Red Tories like they protected all middle class wankers.*

*When we go independent and the real voice of the Scottish working class rules supreme, people like you will pay for what you have done. I'm only sorry that you've made it so my brother has to suffer for it as well.*

*Saor Alba*


I'm still struggling to comprehend what I "did to" his brother, but what I understand all too clearly is that somewhere in Scotland a young man is being abused and possibly threatened because he's gay and because he approached me for advice. The abuse and threats are coming from a close relative who is supposed to love him unconditionally, who is supposed to love and support him. That's the reality of life for LGBTI people right here, right now in 2015. The message of a modern tolerant and inclusive Scotland hasn't reached everyone yet. The monsters of the 1980s are still alive and well.

I thought long and hard about whether to publish this piece. I have not named and shamed the homophobe in order to protect his brother's anonymity. I don't want to make things any worse for the guy who contacted me for advice. But on the other hand people who spout bigotry and hatred need to learn that their attitudes are not acceptable in Scotland - irrespective of whether Scotland becomes independent or remains a part of the Union.

I thought about those who will rub their hands with glee at this exposure of bigotry from within the pro-independence camp. But homophobia is no preserve of one side or the other in Scotland's constitutional debate, and by saying nothing I would be complicit in homophobia myself. The painful truth is that there are still Neanderthals who want independence so they can take Scotland back to a mythical past that never existed, people who believe that freedom means the freedom to abuse and to exclude. People who believe that LGBTI Scots are alien intruders, a foreign infection. People whose saor Alba means poor Alba.

Such people do not represent the vast majority of independence supporters. As a movement we have to challenge those offensive and outdated attitudes, we have a duty to speak out and to condemn them. They have no place in Scotland, not now, not in the future, not ever. We stand for freedom, inclusion and equality for all or we stand for nothing. That's our Scotland.

As I was writing this piece, I received another unpleasant reminder of the realities of modern discrimination. I got a phone call from the Metropolitan Police Pension Agency, demanding repayment of £870. My late partner Andy was a retired policeman who died on September 3rd last year, and I contacted the Pensions Agency on the 5th to inform them of his death. However, it turns out that they had paid his pension for September on the 4th, the day after he died, and now they want me to repay the entire sum.

The rules for Metropolitan police pensions state that a spouse only inherits the pension if they married or had a civil partnership with the police officer while the officer was serving in the police. Although Andy and I had been together for many decades, by the time civil partnerships were introduced, he had long since retired. So I don't get to inherit his pension. I accept that, even though I had to give up work to care for him in his last years, and when he died I was left without an income, without a job and without any money. That £870 went towards paying the costs of Andy's funeral.

But what sticks in my craw is that if we had been a married heterosexual couple who had been together the same length of time that Andy and I had been a couple, the Met Police Pensions Agency would currently be paying me a police widowers pension, instead they are pursuing me for money. So even now, all these years later, homophobia and discrimination still affects me.

I am not going to make it easy for them, but I will probably have to repay the money eventually - the rules are very clear and legally I don't have a leg to stand on. Morally however, I stand strong, and I'll continue to resist and challenge homophobia whatever its source.

What makes it easier is that I know I am not alone.

**Support and advice:**

**The LGBT Helpline Scotland,** call 0300 123 2523

Open every Tuesday and Wednesday between 12 - 9pm

We provide information and emotional support to lesbian, gay, bisexual and transgender people and their families, friends and supporters across Scotland. We are also here to support those questioning or wanting to discuss their sexuality or gender identity.

http://www.lgbt-helpline-scotland.org.uk/

**Equality Network**

Equality Network is Scotland's national lesbian, gay, bisexual, transgender and intersex (LGBTI) equality and human rights charity.

http://www.equality-network.org

**Parents Enquiry Scotland**

Parents Enquiry Scotland is a voluntary organization which provides information and support for parents whose sons or daughters have come out as lesbian, gay, bisexual or transgender. It has been in existence for over 30 years. We offer a range of information leaflets and booklets in addition to our helplines.

http://www.parentsenquiryscotland.org/

**LGBT Youth Scotland**

LGBT Youth Scotland is the largest youth and community-based organisation for lesbian, gay, bisexual and transgender (LGBT) people in Scotland. The charity's mission is to:

"empower lesbian, gay, bisexual and transgender young people and the wider LGBT community so that they are embraced as full members of the Scottish family at home, school and in every community."

https://www.lgbtyouth.org.uk

**Update**

I was later contacted by the young man to say that he had moved in with his sister and was in a safe place.

## Anna Does a Soubry

*5 June 2015*

Scotland's facing a cut of £178 million to its budget, the Labour party are still acting like pettit lipped weans and are refusing to support any SNP anti-austerity amendments, but what certain sections of the media want to talk about is that Alicsammin made a sexist remark. During a particularly tetchy exchange in the Commons over Scottish membership of the Commons Health Committee, Tory minister for small business Anna Soubry was acting like a complete and utter dickhead and giving a masterclass in over the top histrionics, refusing to acknowledge that Scotland has a case for representation on the committee. This resulted in an exasperated Alicsammin snapping at her - "Behave yourself, woman."

The condemnatory headlines were predictable, and they weren't condemning Anna Soubry for acting like a Tory dickhead, even though she was indeed acting like a Tory dickhead and has a long previous history of acting like a Tory dickhead. In fact, if you look up the word soubry in a dictionary of political slang you'll find that it is defined as "over the top Tory dickheadery". As in - that No Borders video during the independence referendum was a bit of a soubry. The infamous incident on Andrew Marr's telly show during the election campaign, when

199

Soubry was being interviewed alongside Alicsammin and slid uncomfortably along the sofa like he was going to infect her with ebola was yet another instance of Anna doing a soubry.

In her exchange with Alicsammin in the Commons, Anna was abusing her position of power as a government minister in order to interrupt and demean. She was doing a soubry. She was in fact abusing her power as a member of a UK government which has little support in Scotland and using it as a means of goading a Scottish MP and taunting him, reminding him of Scotland's subservient position in the Union. Scotland is the powerless one in the soubry equation.

Anna does her soubries as a means of unsettling her opponents and causing them to make mistakes. Unfortunately, Alicsammin fell for it, and in his perfectly justifiable irritation with Anna doing a soubry he was not as careful in his use of language as he should have been. Irrespective of the intent behind it or the circumstances which led to it, when a man snaps at a woman, "Behave yourself woman" - it sounds sexist.

But explaining and investigating the intent and circumstances which led to the remark is precisely what the UK media is not going to do. SNPbad, SNP always bad. And now instead of investigating why a UK government minister thinks it's perfectly fine to abuse her position of power as a means of putting Scotland back in the shortbread tin, we are instead being invited to sympathise with her as a victim of everyday sexism. No one in the mainstream media has bothered to explain why it's vital that Scotland has representation on the Health Committee - even though health is a devolved matter - because the setting of the health budget in England has a direct effect on the health budget for Scotland. Instead all we get is Alicsammin sexist and Scottish meddling in English matters.

The episode is a timely warning to the 56 SNP MPs that the UK media is never ever going to give them the benefit of any doubt. Some in the Scottish independence camp have tried to argue that Alicsammin's remark and his intentions were not sexist, but they're missing the point. The point is that the remark can easily be interpreted as sexist, and when something is capable of being interpreted in a way which is negative for the SNP, and especially Alicsammin, that's exactly what the UK media and establishment is going to do. SNPbad, SNP always bad. In this case, Alicsammin gave them an easy target.

The media boys who cried wolf have tried to broaden their attack - wondering aloud why Alicsammin's remark hasn't been roundly condemned by pro-independence supporters. If the media had responded with equal vigour during the last Parliament to the far worse incidence of sexist bullying directed against a female SNP MP, when Ian Davidson threatened Elidh Whiteford, then perhaps they might now be justified in their attempt to occupy the moral high ground. But we don't have a media which did that, we have a media which goes out of its way to invent entirely spurious attacks on the SNP. There was the entirely invented seatgate affair, there were the allegations that the SNP candidate for Edinburgh South called all No voters quislings when all he did was to post a link to a satirical BBC Scotlandshire article about Unionist politicians. But these lies are still being repeated as though they were true. SNP supporters have been subjected to a barrage of reports about SNPbad, and the media has long since used up its quota of SNP condemned.

In the cosmic scheme of everyday sexism, what Alicsammin said was hardly a ravenous patriarchal wolf who was going to ravage the village. It was more a wee yappy Yorkie biting the ankles of a privileged and powerful woman. Yet now the focus is on what Alicsammin said, and not on the soubry which provoked it. In the UK media everyday sexism trumps everyday Tory privilege and Scotophobia every day, at least when it can be used to attack the SNP.

That's a real and serious issue. By indulging itself in a long and increasingly ridiculous series of unfounded attacks upon the SNP, the mainstream media has now destroyed its own credibility. Should at some time there arise a genuine and serious reason for criticising the SNP and investigating their behaviour, thousands of otherwise perfectly reasonable and fair minded people are not going to listen and are not going to be interested in the media reports. The media has lied, exaggerated, and misled too often. We have a mainstream media that's unfit for purpose.

Meanwhile what gets lost is something that's far more offensive than Alicsammin and the soubry. Scotland's budget being slashed by £178 million and our schools and hospitals being put at risk by a multimillionaire.

What's more offensive is that the Labour party is still bent on acting like a spoiled child who's had its ball taken away from it instead of growing some balls and collaborating actively with the 56 SNP MPs to challenge Tory austerity plans. The real offence is lost in the media fluff, vulnerable people in marginalised communities suffer, and the mainstream media continues to get a free pass and doesn't do its job. That offends me far more than anything Alicsammin said to Anna Soubry.

## Anent the Scotland Bill an Torie Tumshies

*9 June 2015*

Ah thocht, fur a wee chynge, ah'd screive a wee airticle in Scots. Scots an the Gaelic is baith aiquallie Scots leids, an baith hae the exack same richt til the title naciounal leid. Scotland is unique amangst the kintras o Europe kis we hae twa leids o wur ain. Sae ah decidit tae yuise yae o thaim. Aye, we maun be inclusive an apen tae aa at comes tae byde in Scotland an maks this kintra thair hame - kis that is richt an proper. But that disnae mean we maun forget we hae leids an a culture at belangs tae Scotland an aa, else we forget whit maks Scotland Scotland an we hae naethin tae share or tae learn tae the fowk at comes here tae mak Scotland thair hame. Sae here we gang ...

Yestreen in the Hous o Commons in Westminster they debatit the new Scotland Bill. Or raither, they debatit the new Scotland Bill in atweish the Torie tumshies at wis speirin important questiouns anent devolucioun fur Derby or the lamentacious state o street lichts in Letchfield. An thaim at did mynd at they were ther tae debate a Scots maitter thocht that meant myndin thair honourable freins at the SNP wis verra, gey, awfie, bad. They hope that if they repeat it aften enou than fowk in Scotland wull trew thaim, akis that's warkit sae weill fur thaim aa up tae nou.

Mynd, the Shadae Scotland Secretarie - he's cryed shadae akis he's got nae substance - Ian Murray the honourable member fur Red Morningside wis nae better. He wis anither at thocht at he wis ther tae talk aboot hoo bad the SNP is. The debate gied the anerlie Labour MP fae Scotland the chaunce tae explein Labour's new Scots policie, that is "SNP BAD!!" wi capital letters and twa exclamacioun mairks - akis juist the yae wisnae enou. He wis helped bi monie Torie intervenciouns that gaed alang the lines o "Can my honourable friend clarify whether the SNP is bad, very bad, really bad, or pure dead minging?"

An the Labour - Torie tag team birled roun an roun in its glorious irrelevance an anither wee tait o Scots faith in the Westminster seistem deed. They juist cannae help thairsels.

We'r telt bi the Westminster govrenment at the new Scotland Bill wull mak Scotland the maist pouerfu devolved kintra in the warld. An this wad be true, bit anerlie gin maist devolved is defined as - "Whitivver Westminster wants tae gie us. Nou sit doun an eat yer devosupermax wheetos." Kis ther monie ither kintras an regiouns o the warld at haes monie mair pouers nor whit Scotland gets fae this Bill. In feck, ther mair pouerfu municipalities.

The Basque Kintra haes fou fiscal autonomie aareddies. The Basque govrenment collecks aa thair ain taxes an sends the pairt due tae Madrid fur tae pey fur non-devolved pouers tae the central govrenment. An alang wi Catalunya the Basques haes control o broadcastin.

Catalunya haes its ain 24 hour dedicatit news channel, Scotland gets Reporting Scotland an Jackie Bird.

An it's no juist the Basque Kintra an Catalunya at haes thair ain state television, ower in the faur Eist o Europe in Moldova, the puirest kintra in the hale o the continent, ther a wee penkle o territorie cryed Gagauzia at's weer nor Fife. They're yae o the smaaest naciouns in Europe, ther 140,000 ethnic Gagauz, a fowk at's Turkish bi leid an Orthodox Christian bi religioun. The Moldovan constitucioun kens the richt tae autonomie o the Gagauz, an gies thaim wald o thair ain launds, economie, schuils, taxacioun, an broadcastin an aa. They hae thair ain TV channel. Nou mibbies it's no gey guid. Ah widnae ken seein as hou Ah cannae speak Gagauz, tho ther maun be monie at wid say at it cannae be muckle warse nor the airheidit muppits on STV Glesca. But the pynt is at the 140,000 fowk at maks the Gagauz nacioun haes thair ain state broadcaster - somethin at the British govrenment winna allou tae the five million fowk in Scotland.

The Gagauz disnae hae yle, they dinnae hae renewable energie resources, they dinnae hae the win at Scotland haes. But the pynt is that control ower broadcastin has naethin tae dae wi the siller, an ivvriething tae dae wi wha hauds poleitickal control. A wee tait o laund in the puirest kintra o Europe - an it's mair devolved nor Scotland. In the een o Westminster, Scots cannae be lippent tae tell ilka ither the news. We'll mibbies tell truiths at Westminster disnae want us tae hear.

It's no juist broadcastin whaur Westminster shaws it winna lippen Scotland. In monie o the airticles o the new

Scotland Bill, the new devolved pouers kin anerlie be yuised efter speirin permissioun fae wee Fluffie Mundell, the saft toy Paddington Bear o poleiticks. A man at wis washt up on the steps o Westminster wi a label tied tae his duffel coat sayin "Haw gaunie sumbdie luik efter this Torie." Sae they gied him a joab as Scotland Secretarie, an nou the wee lambie thinks he's important - gumptious, aye. It maun be infectious efter sharin a buroo wi Alistair Carmichael.

Wee Fluffie swerrs blin at ther nae veto in the Scotland Bill. Ther is but. The Bill says at the Scotland Secretarie maun gie permissioun onless ther guid raison no tae, but it's left tae the British govrenment tae decern whit's raisonable an whit's no. That gies thaim a hail muckle elastick inch they kin streitch tae a mile.

Sae the truith aboot this bill is that Westminster disae see hit as a wey o giein mair pouer tae Scotland, they see it as a wey o pittin the hems on the SNP. The Scotland Bill, it's no aboot youse, it's no aboot me. It's aboot Westminster haudin the reins o pouer ticht an no lattin thaim drap.


penkle - scrap, small piece of something

wald - control

lippen - to trust, have faith in

gumptious - self-important

decern - determine, decree

win - wealth, wages, profit

trew - believe

## The People vs. Carmichael

*9 June 2015*

Congratulations are due to the Orkney people who have started a fundraiser to get the ruinously expensive funds together to take Aliestair Carmichael, Lib Dem MP for Oh-Are-You-Still-Here-Then, to court and to challenge his election. The fundraiser has now reached its target of £60,000, but it's still possible that legal costs could exceed that amount and there are still two weeks to run on the fundraising period. So if you can, dip into your pocket and give a wee bit. We don't want the four Orkney petitioners to risk their homes and financial security for bravely challenging the supposed right of our political masters to lie, cheat and smear and to treat us like voting sheep they can take for granted. They're not just doing this in order to hold their own MP to account, they're doing it to hold all MPs to account. And Westminster MPs have a long and inglorious track record in unaccountability.

Aliestair has now submitted his legal defence for the case being started against him by a group of pissed off constituents. The shameless MP for Still-Hasn't-Resigned is going for the Andy Coulson defence - Yes I lied, but it was a lie about something else so nyah nyah nyah. In legal parlance this is known as the defensa colli orichalci or the brass neck defence. It's a taunting defence, a

209

defence that's not really a defence, more a statement that you can do what you like and are beyond mere trifles like telling the truth to your electorate. So you can see why it's the kind of defence that a lying politician would be drawn to like a Labour MP to a John Lewis list.

The politicians who write our laws have in their wisdom decided not to make it an offence for a politician to lie to the people who elect them. Isn't that convenient? You could almost believe that they'd set things up that way on purpose. But they wouldn't do that would they? Instead what they've done is to frame the law in such a way that only certain types of lie under certain circumstances are a breach of electoral law. The challenge for the Orkney Four's legal team will be to show that Aliestair's lie falls into these narrowly defined grounds.

The former Scotland Secretary's legal defence is a bit like saying that you are not guilty of a charge of bank robbery because you were out of your tree on heroin and out dogging in the bushes in the park and cheating on your partner at the time, and so were unavailable to drive the getaway car even if you were capable of doing so. This might get you off the charge you're facing, but it's not going to do a whole lot to portray you as a pillar of moral rectitude and a stalwart of community standards. But then Aliestair isn't a pillar of moral rectitude, he's a Lib Dem MP who's only managed to cling on as an MP because he smeared and lied.

Aliestair has previously stated in his defence that he doesn't think he should be judged on the lie and the smear, he should be judged on his record as a constituency MP. He wants us all to draw a discreet veil over his career as a cabinet minister on account of it being an unmitigated disaster. Before getting the Scotland Secretary gig, Aliestair was best known for his pomposity and the bicycle pump up his backside which inflated his ego. He briefed against Michael Moore, the previous Scotland Secretary, and angled for Mikey's job claiming that a bruiser was needed to take on the SNP, and then he was slaughtered by Nicola Sturgeon in the famous debate where he had to beg Rona Dougall to intervene and protect him. And that was the highlight of his ministerial career. That was what he was going to be remembered for before now, when he'll be remembered for the lie and the smear.

He's toxic now. During the recent debate in the Commons on the Scotland Bill he did actually make an intervention. No one responded to it, no one commented on it. Instead he was avoided like a plague carrier. Even those who defended him don't want to be associated with him. Normally you'd feel sad at the poor little party balloon, wafting all alone in the corner. But no one feels sorry for Aliestair, he's brought it all on himself.

The other plank in the strategy to keep Aliestair in his job is for him to keep out of the public eye in the hope that the little people, the wee electoral sheep like you and me, will get fed up and wander off. Being evil cybernats we have short attention spans and will soon go and do something else, like kicking bins over or sending nasty tweets to JK Rowling. After a month or so we'll have forgotten entirely who Aliestair is, and he can return to the pompous obscurity which defined his parliamentary career before he humiliated himself with Rona Dougall.

But we're not going to go away. This is not about vindictiveness, this is not the unjustified mob pursuit of a poor blameless soul. This is about holding the powerful to account, about ensuring that our political masters adhere to the same standards of honesty and integrity that they expect of the rest of us. If a person cannot do their job without lying, cheating, and smearing, then they cannot do their job at all. And when their job entails setting the rules and determining the codes of conduct for everyone else, then there is absolutely no excuse whatsoever for the kind of underhand and duplicitous behaviour evinced by certain politicians.

We have a moral obligation to hold them to account. Because if our legislators have no morals, neither do our laws or our society. That's not the kind of country we should aspire to live in, and it's not the kind of country we will tolerate. That's why what the Orkney Four are doing on all our behalf is so important, and why they deserve our wholehearted support.

## OBR – Osborne's Basketcase Reasons

*11 June 2015*

'm still struggling with the premise of the Unionist argument against Full Fiscal Autonomy. When the UK runs a deficit, this is normal, but if Scotland were to do it it would be the end of civilisation as we know it and fiscalmageddon. We'd be so poor that we'd have to sleep in a drawer alongside Jim Murphy, and you'd all be sorry then Scottish nationalist types. You wouldn't even be able to afford the bill for the counselling you'd require because the NHS won't cover it. Funny how no one asks whether the UK and its permadecifit can afford to be fiscally autonomous. Apparently that's different - just because - right. Now shut up and eat your wheatos.

Clearly, like the country I come from, I'm too stupid to understand why we're too poor and too wee. Not like the OBR, which is supposed to stand for the Office for Budget Responsibility but where Scotland is concerned really stands for Osborne's Basketcase Reasons. Osborne's Basketcases can always give Reasons why Scotland is too wee, too poor, and too stupid.

Entirely coincidentally and totally independently, the OBR has produced some more figures showing how basketcasish Scotland is on the very day that the SNP table an amendment to the Scotland Bill to give Scotland

Full Fiscal Autonomy. See all that oil in the North Sea? Well now it's worth three buttons, two five Euro cent coins from the back of the sofa, and an ocean of sneers from the UK media. You'll have had your North Sea bonanza then, and it's all been spent on tax cuts for rich people, transport infrastructure for London, and editorials in the Tory press telling Scotland it ought to be grateful. We should be feeling suitably chastised by now.

In what was described as a significant blow against Scotland's hopes for Full Fiscal Autonomy, the OBR has revised its forecast for oil taxation revenues from £37 billion to a mere £2 billion, downgrading their previous prediction by a factor of 17.5. Which if you ask me sounds rather more like a significant blow against the prediction credibility of the OBR.

Whether Scotland can afford FFA depends in no small part on what Scotland will be spending its money on. Let's leave aside the fact that the Unionist parties appear to believe that under FFA Scotland would still be paying a share of England only projects like the high speed railway line between London and Birmingham, London Crossrail, and the lovely new London sewer. Let's leave aside that the financial arguments are predicated on a fiscally autonomous Scotland maintaining Tory spending plans. Let's leave aside the unseemly pleasure they take from the supposed fact that they have left the country that they have governed for decades a helpless basketcase which can't pay it's own way in the world. Labour and the Tories ruled Scotland for decades, they gloat about how poor Scotland is, and then they wonder why people don't want to vote for them. Now that's the

Unionist version of too wee too poor stupid, a special kind of small minded poverty of spirit stupid.

But that's not what gets me. Even that heady hypocrisy is not what gets my goat and makes me hurl a shoe at the telly in a howl of helplessness. What really gets me is the Groundhog Day of it all, the never ending circularity of pointless mediocrity. The grinding round and down of the Westminster millstone on Scottish expectations. We are constantly told that we have an unsustainable deficit and Scotland's is greater and less sustainable than most. And having produced this state of affairs the Unionists cry that this is precisely the reason why things should forever remain unchanged and the people who lumbered us with this unsustainable deficit should keep their jobs and keep producing the unsustainability. Producing unsustainability is apparently the only thing that the Unionist parties can reliably sustain.

The Unionist parties offer no way out of this cycle of despair and circle of hell. They have no small ideas, never mind big ones. There are no dreams, no plans, no proposals, not even a whiff of a suggestion. There is nothing in their box of miserabilist tricks which proposes a means of growing Scotland's economy out of the dependency which they tell us they have created for us. There are no answers from them about our ageing population, about what to do when the oil runs out, or how to maintain our public services without the handouts they insist we need from London's financial sector.

We're too wee, too poor, and too stupid and are doomed to remain so for ever more. The Unionist parties need Scotland to remain in this lamentable state so that they can score rhetorical points off the SNP. It's the politics of the infant school. On Thursday in the Scottish Parliament, the Labour party insisted that Scotland needs the price of oil to be US$200 million per barrel, or some such ludicrous figure. But then this is the party that told us that if they won the election they'd give Scotland 1000 more nurses than the SNP would, irrespective of how many the SNP paid for. So numeracy is clearly not their strong point.

There shouldn't be any argument about this. Scotland has already voted in favour of full fiscal autonomy, or devo max or whatever it's called these days. The electorate of Scotland put their crosses next to the SNP candidate. And by a peculiar quirk of fate, it's the SNP which is the party that campaigned on a manifesto promising Scotland what the Unionist parties promised they'd give us in the frantic final days of the independence referendum.

Actually it's not really a peculiar quirk of fate, it's yet another consequence of the Unionist parties being lying manipulative gits who'll promise absolutely anything and then renege on it. This is not unconnected with the reason why they got slaughtered in the election in Scotland. If they lie repeatedly about what they're going to do in office, they can hardly complain that people in Scotland are increasingly disinclined to believe their dire warnings of full fiscal doom.

# Nous n'habitons pas en Québec

**13 June 2015**

Scotland isn't Quebec. We don't speak French, we think poutine is the homophobic president of Russia, and Celine Dion is not a national hero. And it's because we're not Quebec that Scottish independence is inevitable whereas Quebecois independence is far less certain. This is about the only observation that Gordie Broon got right in his article in the Guardian on Friday, in which he blamed the Tories for the impending demise of the United Kingdom. True to form, Gordie spectacularly failed to recognise his own role in bringing about the end of the Union, but we'll get to that later.

Canada has very good reasons for wanting Quebec to remain a part of Canada. Without Quebec the future of Canada is gravely threatened. Without Quebec, Canada would be divided into two geographically distinct regions 1000 miles apart, and all they'd have to distinguish themselves from their southern neighbours in the USA would be Mounties and Dan Ackroyd.

Since all they'd have would be the less animated Blues Brother, the chances are that one or other of Canada's bits would then decide they might as well apply to become the 51st state, assuming Puerto Rico doesn't beat them to it. This simple geographic truth gives Ottawa an existential reason to want to make sure that

Quebec stays Canadian. Existential, see, that's all Jean Paul Satre-ish, and he was a French speaker too. So it's all tres appropriate. Quebec is all that stops Canada from sitting morosely in a café with a croissant and a Gaulois and debating the meaning of existence.

This doesn't hold true with Scotland and the UK. Should Scotland leave the UK, there is of course no UK anymore, seeing as how the UK was formed by the union of the Kingdom of Scotland and the Kingdom of England and its associated bits. Of course the rest of the UK might very well decide that they were still going to be the UK and no one in Scotland would really bat much of an eyelid. However due to the continuing confusion between the terms England and Britain, the loss of Scotland would not make the UK sit morosely in a café, or even a chip shop.

The point is that England, Wales and Northern Ireland remain England, Wales and Northern Ireland with or without Scotland. The independence of Scotland does not make it likely that Kent might apply to become a part of France. Although they should, if for no other reason than it would really piss off Nigel Farage.

Scottish independence might be a blow to the pride of Westminster, and the loss of Scottish resources a blow to the UK Treasury, but the continuance of Westminster and its Treasury are not threatened in the same way.

All this means that the stakes are far higher for the rest of Canada than they are for the rest of the UK. The Tories can afford to play fast and loose with the Union, and their voters will tolerate it, in a way that isn't politically possible in Canada. Canada has to make accommodations to Quebec because it needs Quebec in order for there still to be a Canada. The UK doesn't have to make the same accommodations to Scotland, and you only have to look at the actions of the Unionist parties over the past thirty years to see that they've given the least amount of devolution possible. And they've given it grudgingly, with immense ill will, and hedged about with caveats, booby traps and restrictions. The Unionist parties have never viewed devolution for Scotland as something that's worthwhile, as something that is a response to the desire of the electorate of Scotland. They've only ever seen it as a political tool for defeating the SNP.

And they're still doing it. Even though the voters of Scotland have dumped a bucket of ice cold SNP water over their heads, the Unionist parties have still not woken up. They're still playing the party politics game, they're still viewing devolution as a tool to use to defeat the SNP and not as an answer to the legitimate demands of the voters of Scotland. We've told them we want devo max, but they're still not listening.

And that's the big blind spot in Gordie's rant that the Tories are risking the Union. Gordie has been equally guilty in Union risking. If he'd really been so concerned about the future of the UK you'd think that once he was no longer burdened with the demands of high office on his time and he returned to the back benches he might have made it his mission. But he didn't. He couldn't even be bothered to turn up. You'd think he might just have done something about it when he was Prime Minister, or when he was Chancellor of the Exchequer. But he didn't.

He was too interested in plotting and smearing his way into the top job to worry about what he was going to do once he got there and was quite happy to impose a form of devolution that was designed to provide Labour with a Parliament it could still be in power in even if the Tories returned to power in Westminster. That was Labour's thinking in 1997, and now Gordie is upset because it's bitten Labour on the bum.

Now that Gordie is no longer in office and no longer has to turn up to anything, he wants everyone else to turn up to a convention so everyone else can do what Gordie should have done twenty years ago, and devise a lasting settlement for the Union. He even thinks the SNP should be invited, so that's nice. But it's not going to happen, because the SNP have nothing to gain from helping Labour devise a constitutional settlement to keep the Union, the Lib Dems don't exist anymore, Labour is a headless chicken and the Tories still don't need to listen. It's too little, too late, *parce que nous n'habitons pas en Québec.*

**Bye Bye Jim**

*13 June 2015*

B ye bye Jim Murphy, he shall coyote no more and shall be sadly missed by a couple of dozen parody accounts on Twitter. Jim has finally given up the leadership of the Labour party in Scotland, or to be more accurate, it was clawed out of the cold dead hands of his extinct career by the sheer and utter ignominy of the deep dark chasm into which he's thrown the party. It's a defeat from which Labour may never recover, and Jim has secured himself a small footnote in the annals of Scottish political history as the man who made Michael Forsyth look like he was competent.

Forward thinking, dignified and statesmanlike, analytic in his searing political insights, and generous and magnanimous in spirit - these are just a few of the descriptions that no one would ever use with reference to Jim. He won't be missed by the punters, although he will be missed by the SNP. His resignation is the first major setback that Nicola Sturgeon has faced. Jim's most notable, and indeed only, achievement was being the greatest recruiting tool that the SNP have ever known.

Jim's a political magician, he made the Labour party disappear. He clawed his way into the leadership after briefing against and undermining Johann Lamont in private, combined with pious and sanctimonious statements in public condemning Labour infighting. It was the aftermath of the referendum and Labour was staring disaster in the face. But Jim had stood on an Irn Bru crate and bravely faced down an egg, and he was confident that he could turn around the party's fortunes. True to his word Jim did exactly that, he turned the party round.

Unfortunately he turned them round so that they were staring at an apocalypse and an extinction level event. Asteroids hurtling to the ground at 60,000 mph have been less destructive to the survival prospects of dinosaurs, and Jim managed an almost total wipe out of Labour's expensaurus wrecks. It really would be fitting if, in tribute to Jim's service to dinosaur extinction, an airless barren rock orbiting in the cold dark lonely depths of space where no one ever visits and no life is to be found was to be named after him. After all, that's a pretty accurate description of Labour's Scottish headquarters now that Jim has worked his magic.

Jim's resignation speech was notable mainly for its digs at Alicsammin. Jim slated the former First Minister for not shutting up and going away and crawling under a rock, but of course there isn't enough space there what with all the former Labour MPs scurrying out of the light. And of course there is also the consideration that whereas Alicsammin is universally hailed as one of the most competent and capable politicians in the UK, most Labour MPs from Scotland were never capable of joined up sentences, or indeed joined up thinking, to begin with.

That's what I will miss most about Jim. Alicsammin is an arrogant politician, but he's an arrogant politician who has got a great deal to be arrogant about. Jim matched him in arrogance but there was nothing behind it except Jim's estimation of himself and the vacuous bubble of media hype. That's the mismatch that makes Jim God's gift to satire. The media was convinced that Jim was going to put the fear of Gord into the SNP, and the howls of derisory laughter from independence supporters were really an attempt to hide how afraid we were of Jim's galactic abilities. But in fact they were just howls of derisory laughter.

Ostensibly the resignation speech was a speech about the way forward for the Labour party. After losing the party all but one of its seats in what was formerly regarded as its homeland and impregnable stronghold, for some bizarre reason Labour thinks that the guy who threw the party off a cliff is the best person to develop a strategy for them to move forward. It's a bit like trusting a financial advisor who bet all your money on a blind three legged horse to restore your fortunes because this time round a drunk journalist in the pub has told him about a three legged horse with one eye. But then you really shouldn't believe anything you read in the Daily Mail, believing what the Daily Mail says has been Labour's downfall.

Jim does have a bright idea. He's used the past month well and scribbled down a few ideas that a GCSE politics student could have come up with on the bus into school after spending the night out on the town instead of doing

223

their homework. And appropriately enough a GCSE is also Jim's highest educational qualification.

Now, because he believes the Daily Mail, he's spotted a one-eyed three legged horse with its snout firmly ensconced in the trough. The bright idea is for Labour to open up the party list for Holyrood MSPs so the MPs who lost their seats in May can get back on the gravy train again. Because what Labour really needs right now is a bunch of discredited politicians that the voters kicked out of office just a few weeks ago. Jim managed to screw up the pitiful remnants of the Labour party, and he's determined to ensure that it continues along the same miserable path.

He's set his face against Labour in Scotland becoming a Scottish Labour party, ensuring that it will continue to ride on the coat tails of a UK party that is drifting ever rightwards in search of votes in leafy constituencies in Toryshire. But then Jim always did approve of Labour's drift to the right, his great mistake was to imagine that he could take the rest of us with him.

It's really very simple what Labour's plan ought to be in Scotland. They should study very carefully what Jim has done. They should look upon his tenure in office and examine it in detail. They should list each of his actions and policy announcements. And then they should do the exact opposite.

Bye bye Jim. You won't be missed.

## Labour's Number 2s

*15 June 2015*

This article should have been published a few hours ago, but when I heard the news that Gordon Matheson thought he could be a great deputy leader for the Labour party in Scotland I had to go and change my underwear because I was laughing so much.

The Labour leadership contest in Scotland has only just started, and it's already descended into farce. Concerned that the resignation of Jim Murphy had left Scotland's satirists and twitter parodists without a suitably balloon like target for their ridicule, the always reliable Labour party has stepped up to the plate and provided us with the zeppelin ego of Gordon Matheson. Just as Jeremy Corbyn is a no hoper on the UK leadership ticket as a service to Labour to disguise the fact that it is now a right wing party, the leader of Glesca Cooncil has likewise announced his intention to stand as a no hoper on the deputy leader ticket as a service to Labour, because this will disguise the fact that the other candidates are deeply unappealing and implausibly ridiculous buffoons as well.

Wee Gordie's announcement is not, and I repeat not, remotely connected with any new Labour rule that the deputy leader gets prime billing in the list for the Scottish elections next year and will be virtually guaranteed an

MSP seat. How could you possibly imagine that the leader of Glesca Cooncil could ever contemplate being self-serving.

Well I say announced, in fact Wee Gordie shouted it excitedly like a demented garden gnome on speed. After all this is a man who almost wet himself with excitement on witnessing John Barrowman's performance at the opening of the Commonwealth Games and forgot that microphones had been invented. These were games which, we were told, were going to bring lasting benefits to the people of the East End of Glasgow, and which gave us a swimming pool and a park. Only now we're told that the park in Dalmarnock is to be sold off to property developers - the only people who have gained lasting cash based benefits, as indeed they have been throughout Labour's decades in power in Glasgow.

Glesca Labour likes to sell things off. They've rezoned public parks allowing them to rent them out for corporate events, and now they're hell bent on removing the steps on Buchanan Street, one of the few public spaces in the city centre, because what the city centre really needs is more retail units.

Wee Gordie's candidacy brings a number of advantages. The other big advantage of course is that unlike Labour MSPs who will struggle to stay in post in less than a year's time, Wee Gordie is a cooncillor and will still have a job all the way through to 2017. This also proves that, contrary to popular belief, a coffin can indeed have more than one last nail. Wee Gordie is the B&Q of last nails, supplying a huge selection of last nails to suit all of

226

Labour's coffin requirements. He can bury Labour more deeply than the Scottish media buried the true story of his predecessor's fall from grace.

Wee Gordie took over leadership of Glesca Cooncil after its previous leader self-destructed in a cocaine based frenzy in ways never properly investigated by Scotland's media. But then not properly investigating the goings on in Glesca Cooncil is a Scottish media tradition as hoary as seven days hard with Francis Gay. Back in the 1961, the Italian conceptual artist Piero Manzoni canned his crap and sold it as art, he got the idea from Glesca Cooncil, which has been canning crap and selling it to the Glesca public for far longer. Now Wee Gordie has taken the concept to its logical conclusion and wants to be Labour's number 2s. There are those of us who'd suggest that he already has been for quite a long time.

Wee Gordie says he has a track record in success - but since he successfully body swerved Labour's cooncil manifesto commitment to introduce free city wide wi-fi, no one can Google it to find out so we're expected just to take his word for it. Wee Gordie's wi-fi track record probably disappeared down the non-existent tunnels of the East End Subway extension that the party promised when they were touting for the Commonwealth Games.

It should be pointed out, in the interests of fairness, that Glesca Cooncil has been promising an extension of the Subway into the East End since the 1940s. It took Labour almost 100 years from the foundation of the party to 1997 to fulfil its promise of a Scottish Parliament, so it's

227

unfair to expect the Subway extension any time before 2040.

Amongst Wee Gordie's other achievements is the competition to revamp George Square. The design that the other judges favoured lost out because Wee Gordie didn't like it, so he cancelled the competition at a cost to the public which ran into the tens of thousands. Apparently the favourite design wasn't suitable for citrus based celebrations and didn't provide enough landing space for zeppelin sized egos floating above lawn ornament sized bodies.

It's just as well that the out-going leader of Labour in Scotland has said that Scottish politics have a "post-truth" atmosphere. Labour ought to know all about that, as they took truth and blew it into a thousand pieces with just about every blood stained Iraqi press release that ever issued from the offices of John McTernan and Alistair Campbell.

Gordon Matheson has been an enthusiastic exponent of the Labour art of removing truth from public statements and leaving only truthiness. It's his ability to fabricate dissembling out of collected bits and pieces of rubbish like an over-egged womble that's his main, his only, selling point.

For the SNP and the Greens, who are rapidly gaining credibility as the replacement for Labour as the main opposition party in Scotland, a Labour party led by Kezia Dugdale with Gordon Matheson as her deputy must be all their Christmases at once.

See that. I got through an entire one thousand word article about how the SNP and the Greens are the only people who are going to be thankful that Gordon Matheson wants to be the deputy leader of the Labour Party in Scotland - and I didn't even mention dogging and car parks. Apart from just there.

## The American Tea of Politics

*28 June 2015*

Well that's me home now. Big thanks to Macart and all the people who published guest posts during my absence and kept the shop open. I appreciate it immensely. I forgot my phone charger so decided just to switch it off when leaving Heathrow and spent the entire holiday incommunicado. On reflection, that was a better idea. Being disconnected from electronic devices meant I was really able to relax and forget about everything. But I'm back now, refreshed and opinionated as ever.

I had a wonderful time in Boston, doing all the usual touristy stuff. It's an easy city to discover on foot. The food was great. I've now acquired a new love for Vietnamese food. I met up with an old friend and had a fantastic time with him. He's the self-confessed world's worst tour guide, but great company, and didn't even complain when I insisted on dragging him to the nether end of Boston's public transport system so I could have a ride on an old fashioned streetcar.

I also discovered the real reason why they threw all that tea into Boston harbour and sparked off the American Revolution. It wasn't a principled stand against unfair taxation, oh no. It was really because American tea is seriously howffstrous, boakalicious, and just plain boggin. You'd think that a nation that put a man on the moon might have grasped the simple concept of putting the teabag in the cup before you add boiling water, but seemingly this is beyond the wit of a country with drive in funeral parlours. Probably saying this makes me an evil Scottish cybernat, but apparently evil Scottish cybernat racism only counts as evil Scottish cybernat racism when you tell jokes about English people while in pursuit of Scottish independence, so I reckon I am on safe ground here slagging off American tea making abilities. Although with the Daily Mail you can never be sure. Americans don't count as foreigners to the Daily Mail, at least not the white, heterosexual, English speaking ones, even if they can't make a decent cup of tea.

One trendy "tea bar" near Harvard Yard asked if I wanted boba in my tea. I thought that was Michael Jackson's pet chimpanzee, but apparently it's some sort of tapioca. Seemingly people with ironic beards like that sort of thing. Anyway, I politely declined the cuppa semolina chimp, and told the server I just wanted a common or garden cup of hot tea - because by this time I'd worked out that if you ask an American for tea you're quite likely to get given something with ice in it. And then I got presented with a cup of tepid water to which a tea bag had been briefly introduced. To be honest, the chimpanzee would have tasted better, which is probably why Michael Jackson got him in the first place.

So there you have it. America got its separation from the UK because their tea is crap. Not any high principled stuff about taxation or democracy. Perhaps we could take a tealeaf from the Americans' book and start a Scottish revolution by demolishing the BBC Scotland headquarters and chucking the pieces into what used to be the harbour at Pacific Quay, not because the licence fee is an unfair tax and obligatory state sponsored propaganda is profoundly undemocratic, but because River City is a bit rubbish.

So while I was away out of touch with Caledonian civilisation and being offered bowffericious tannin based beverages while learning about their relationship to revolution, Clypegate happened. The Labour party in Scotland is in a death spiral, it's already bouncing off the treetops and about to plunge into a deep ravine and explode in a shower of spangly Blair McDougalls, so you'd imagine that any party in such a dire set of circumstances would be taking a long hard look at itself and considering fundamental changes to the way it has operated all these years. But no. Labour thinks it just needs to keep on doing the exact same thing, only more so. Because that's really going to work for them.

Labour has stared defeat in the face, and it's crapping itself. Having scrapped any form of socialism that the party once possessed it's no longer a Labour movement but a bowel movement. Now it's decided to use the Daily Mail to help it spread the keech about a bit.

Personally, as an evil cybernat, I was devastated to discover that I wasn't named by the Daily Mail. I'd say named and shamed but I was born without the shame gene. And I'm so evil I throw jeely pieces out of windaes, and the pieces don't have any jeely on them. That's pure evil that is. However it's not as pure evil as the Labour party, which is pure evil combined with pathetic and disgusting and has long since gone off the boil, a bit like American tea really. There's a real insult there - far worse than calling them traitors, the Labour party are the American tea of politics.

I'm not taking it personally, as the real reason I've not been named and unshamed is because I'm not an SNP member so there's no political mileage in it. You can't scream SNP accused at a person who's not answerable to the SNP. Although I'm sure that wouldn't stop them trying.

However, it's unlikely that there's a great deal of mileage for Labour in screaming SNP accused at people on Twitter who are SNP members. It's not like this is a tactic that they've never tried before and represents a new strategy which will turn around their fortunes. Labour's staff members and its few remaining politicians have been trolling the nation for years now and screaming SNP accused at every opportunity - aided and abetted by their friends in an increasingly discredited and discreditable media. And look where it's got them.

I thought Blair McDougall was supposed to be a master strategist? I suppose he is if you want a strategy for disappearing down the nearest stank. And to put the yellow ice on the crapcake, what Labour has done might even be illegal and a breach of the Data Protection Act. It is not illegal to call a politician a traitor. It's a robust opinion, and robust opinions are what democracy is founded upon. The American revolutionaries understood that one, even if they didn't know how to make a decent cuppa.

So to those souls how have been demonised by the Daily Mail for calling someone a traitor, wear it with pride. It means you've annoyed someone. And that's a great start for a revolution.

## Being Pecked to Death by an Angry Chicken

*29 June 2015*

Yesterday the Sunday Herald did something that no other newspaper in the UK has ever done before - it carried an article exposing the online activities of the numerous Unionist Twitter trolls. The mainstream media has until now ignored the swearing, threats and abuse originating from those who support the Union, preferring to concentrate on the portrayal of independence supporters as the agents of an evil nationalist cult, beardy blue face painted Minions in kilts but without the movie deal. While I am glad that a major publication has finally pointed out the obvious - that people are rude on the Internet - I can't help but thinking that it's all a bit petty.

Well I say "a bit", which is like saying that the Labour party in Scotland and dinosaurs are a bit extinct, or that Gordon Matheson is a bit of a car park attendant. But seriously, why should anyone care what a random punter says on Twitter? Although you can understand why Blair McDougall might care, it's not like he's got anything else to do with his time. He was appointed as an advisor to Jim Murphy, but now his job description is "waiting for jotters".

You could quite easily say that being a bit petty is what Twitter is all about. Twitter is the sound-bite generator of the Internet. On Twitter you get 140 characters to express yourself, so you're not going to get subtle and nuanced, it's not bloody Tolstoy. You get LOLZ and abbreviations. You get gross simplification and childishness. Sometimes, if you're lucky, you get funny one liners and you can guarantee there's a lot of pictures of cute kittens. It's a bit like Reporting Scotland without the laughs or the hotline to Labour party press releases, only you're not charged £145 a year for the privilege and it's easier to ignore the fitba references.

And occasionally, but thankfully rarely, you get really nasty individuals who vilify and traduce, abuse and traduce, post people's home addresses and threaten them - usually women - with violence and rape. This sort of behaviour is of course illegal and it is a criminal offence. But what the Murphoid remnants of the Labour party have been trying to do is to conflate the robust expression of political opinion with criminal threats to hunt down a woman and rape her. They've been engaged in a deliberate campaign to leech on the very real abuse faced by some people on the Internet and sook oot what sympathy they can from it. And the mainstream media has been egging them on.

We are where we are because the mainstream media has made such a big play of supposed abuse by independence supporters and ignored the abuse originating from Unionists. The result is that you can read just about any report on Scotland in the majority of the UK press and it's like being pecked to death by an irate chicken, only with a lower IQ and a greater amount of hysteria. Although on reflection that's being unfair to chickens. Chickens don't know how to lie. Half the time what is carried in the media about Scotland is an outright falsehood. If the lying lurid headlines splashed all over the front pages ever do get corrected, it's in tiny print in an inside page, hiding below an article about breast enlargement.

And that's even before you venture into the comments section, where there's a den of spittle flecked invective and hatred which would make the average Twitter user rush to cuddle a Minion in comfort. The real issues are lost in a flurry of net curtain twitching and finger pointing. Supporters of the Union don't even address the fundamental contradiction lurking at the very heart of their own argument, it's never been pointed out to them by the press that feeds the flames of hatred and disdain.

Let's accept, for the sake of argument, that Scotland is a basket case which requires the UK in order to keep it from the fate of Greece. Whose fault is that then? Sure as hell it isn't the SNP who have had their paws on the levers of macroeconomic policy for the past century or two. But apparently we're better off remaining under the tender administrations of the maliciously incompetent idiots who have brought about this lamentable state of affairs - reducing what could have been a prosperous northern European country with an embarrassment of natural resources to penury and dependency. That's the core contradiction at the heart of the Unionist argument, and by ignoring it, all that is left is the childish idiocy of finger pointing on Twitter. Pooling and sharing my arse.

So having infantilised and trivialised the debate, then they complain when they're not taken seriously.

They have chosen to infantilise and trivialise the debate on Scottish independence, and by extension fostering the notion that independence is itself an infantile and trivial idea. The underlying message is that if you want Scottish independence then you're trivial, you're obsessed by something that is unimportant and meaningless. And this tells us what the Union thinks about Scotland. It's Scotland that is trivial and unimportant. It's not about self-determination. It's not about democracy. It's not about achieving a cohesive and fair society, redistributing wealth and land, or social justice and equality. It's all about rude names on Twitter and the pursed lips of disapproving prudery.

I want to live in a country which is taken seriously by its politicians and opinion formers, a country which is important to those who take the decisions about its future, a country which is central to the policies of those who determine its economy. But apparently that's too much to ask for in a Scotland which is a part of the UK.

When we get independence we can at least remedy these things. We can have politicians we can hold to account if they don't treat us like adults. But we're probably going to be stuck with a media which trivialises everything unless we build a new one for ourselves.

238

## English Votes for Everyone's Laws

*1 July 2015*

The Tories have decided to rush through a measure which they claim is dedicated to ensuring fairness and equality between the constituent parts of this greatest Union of nations the multiverse has ever seen. It's EVEL, which sounds like a description of the Daily Mail, but which supposedly stands for English votes for English laws. This all sounds just fine and dandy and who could possibly object to it? It's all terribly fair and British and cricket on the lawnish, after all doesn't Scotland have its own parliament and English MPs can't vote on Scottish matters. Why shouldn't England have its say on things which affect it without those uppity Caledonians interjecting in their incomprehensible accents.

But unfortunately it doesn't seem to work like that. Scotland's overall budget is determined by the budget set for England, and when Scotland's MPs can no longer vote on what are supposedly English only matters, they will lose the ability to have a say on the overall budget for Scotland. It's like going to a restaurant and being told that you can order anything you like, as long as it doesn't cost more than what your companion has ordered. They can choose anything they like, and their London transport infrastructure pudding counts as a joint UK national expenditure. And then you get the bill after they've decided that they want privatisation pie with austerity chips.

But it's even worse than that. Scotland doesn't even get to decide what parts of the menu it chooses its cauld porridge from. That is also decided for us by our dining companion. Fancy something full fat fiscal autonomy? Forget it. Tory and Labour MPs we didn't vote for have decided it's bad for us, it will ruin our arteries and give us a sense of independence that's unhealthy. Scotland must restrict itself to the devolved parts of the menu, but it doesn't have any say on what the devolved parts are. That gets decided for us. We only get to choose from the cheap end of the menu, the appetisers and the nibbles, the parts that don't allow a full and satisfying meal. One of those tiny side dishes that has the appearance of a dinner but doesn't contain any calories. Then they can tell us that we've had our chips on our shoulders and we need to stop complaining.

Over 500 non Scottish MPs ganged up to vote down a proposal for full fat fiscal autonomy, the proposal that Scotland voted for at the General Election and which was backed by the overwhelming majority of Scotland's MPs. At the General Election Scotland resoundingly rejected the Smith Proposals as inadequate and derisory and voted for a party that wanted to go much further. And we did so by a landslide.

But this counts for nothing. Westminster and the Unionist parties are stuck on Smith like a fish bone in their throats, even though it's choking them to death. The Labour and Tory MPs clapped and cheered when they told Scotland it couldn't have what it had voted for, like they'd scored a mighty victory. But the only victory is the reminder that England is much larger than Scotland and as long as we remain in this Union we will always be outvoted. Outvoted, unappreciated, unwanted unless we haud oor wheesht like good little North Britons and are grateful for the morsels we're given.

So here we are in the devolution café. English MPs get to decide what parts of the legal menu Scotland can choose from, and English MPs get to decide the overall budgets which form the basis for determining Scottish spending on those parts of the menu that English MPs allow us to choose from. Scotland currently gets outvoted on these things, but at least our MPs have a say. Once the Tories get their way, Scotland's MPs won't even have a vote at all. We'll be silenced and side lined, marginalised and meaningless.

So it's clear that the Tories are also in favour of English votes for Scottish laws, and presumably also English votes for Welsh laws and Northern Irish laws. Given the recent behaviour of the Unionist parties, we now know that EVEL really stands for English votes for everyone's laws. That's democracy Westminster style.

Remember during the independence referendum that Scotland was told, frequently, that it wasn't a colony. Unionists scoffed at the minority of independence supporters who compared Scotland to a colony. And by and large supporters of independence agreed. Of course Scotland wasn't a colony - I agreed with that proposition myself. Scotland was a part of a Union in which we all thought that we had a fair say. A Union not a takeover.

But once Cameron passes his measure to bring in English Votes for Everyone's Laws that won't be the case anymore. Scotland will be without the means to have any say at all over its overall budget, no say on how much it gets for health, no say on how much it gets for education. England's MPs will determine the total budget and Scotland will get its budget decided in a vote from which our own representatives have been excluded. Scotland will get a percentage of whatever is decided for England, but won't be able to have any input into what is decided for England. So if, in a fit of Conservative madness, Tory MPs for England decide to halve the health budget and introduce rampant privatisation, the part of the Scottish block grant accounting for health services will be proportionately slashed too. And there will be nothing we can say or do about it. This is Labour's pooling and sharing, this is Better Together's best of both worlds.

What was that that the Americans once said about no taxation without representation? That's the position the Colony of Scotland will find itself in once EVEL comes into force. We will be a colony, without a say, without a vote, and staring at a menu of stale crumbs that are well past their sell by date with no choice in the matter, no say, no representation. Our MPs will be second class, just like the country that elects them.

Welcome to the Colony of Scotland.

**Bow Down Before Your Imperial Masters**

*2 July 2015*

The House of Commons has a committee which scrutinises Scottish legislation - yeah! Scottish scrutiny for Scottish laws - yeah! And it's even chaired by thon guy that used to be in Run Rig - yeah! Mind you, the committee has almost as many English Tory MPs as it does Scottish MPs - because that's what we voted for at the last election, wasn't it? I distinctly remember Paddington Mundell counting for almost as much as the rest of Scotland's MPs combined, the BBC seems to thinks so. So the fact that the Scottish Affairs Committee is made up of four SNP MPs and three English Conservative MPs is totally fair and balanced right? It's fair in exactly the same way the Iain Duncan Smith's benefits reforms are fair, like Job Centre sanctions are fair. You know, Michael Gove's definition of justice. And he's Scottish, so we can't complain or we're just racists who hate the English.

Anyway, the Tory MPs are outnumbered by the SNP ones, so there's no room on our shoulders for chips. But not to worry, just to make sure that the non-Scottish MPs aren't outnumbered on a committee devoted entirely to Scottish matters and nothing else, it's got three Labour MPs as well, and they are all representing English seats too. It's the flip side of English votes for English laws - it's English votes for Scottish committees.

So in line with the democratic principle of English votes for Scottish affairs, Scotland's MPs are going to be outnumbered on Westminster's only purely Scottish committee by six to four. Still, at least that's not quite as bad as being outnumbered by 600 odd - some of whom are extremely odd, I mean have you seen Michael Fabricant's hair? - to 59 which is what happens in the rest of the parliament. This represents a huge advance for Scottish rights and representation, because now we've only got six imperial masters to bow down before, instead of bowing down before 600, which really does play havoc on the knees.

So who are our Imperial masters who control our destiny but who were foisted upon us without Scotland having any say in the matter? Och silly us, thinking that we should get a majority say on matters that only affect Scotland. Who are these savants who know more about Scotland than any MP who might actually represent a Scottish constituency and have been given their job by voters in Scotland?

Christopher Chope is the Tory MP for Christchurch in Dorset. He's not Scottish, although rumour has it that he did once mistake a grouse beater in Morayshire for a grouse. Christopher's hobbies include scoffing at poor people, revelling in his sense of entitlement, and demonising benefits claimants. So fairly typical for a Tory then. Chris spent the Thatcher years introducing the Poll Tax, so he's got previous experience at opinionating on laws that no one wants and no one voted for. In a previous incarnation he was a colonial governor, just like he is in this one. Chris is in favour of hanging, conscription, and keeping developing countries in hock to banks.

David Anderson is the Labour MP for Blaydon, which is in Tyneside so that's practically in Scotland isn't it? Geordies say things like "doon the toon" so it's more or less the same as being Scottish. And some small parts of David's constituency are actually on the northern side of Hadrian's Wall, so as far as the Daily Mail is concerned that makes him a raving blue face painted Braveheartist. In the real world, he's at best lukewarm on the subject of further devolution for Scotland.

Jim Cunningham is the Labour MP for Coventry South, but he ran away to the bright lights and bustling opportunities of Coventry from Coatbridge. So he is actually Scottish, a Tom Clarke who couldn't make the mark. Jim cares so much about his former homeland that he's been absent from most votes in the Commons on Scottish devolution since 2010 and on the occasions when he has been arsed enough to vote, he's voted against extra devolution almost as much as he's voted in favour. And this guy is the only Scot who's been drafted in to make up numbers.

Stephen Hepburn is the Labour MP for Jarrow, which is also in Tyneside. There's clearly a theme here. It is perfectly possible that no one in London appreciates the difference between Tyneside and Scotland, and thinks that Newcastle is a suburb of Edinburgh. Tynecastle is in

Edinburgh after all, this is probably the source of the confusion.

Dan Poulter is the Tory MP for Central Suffolk and North Ipswich. But Suffolk starts with the letter S, and so does Scotland, so this qualifies him as an expert in all things Caledonian. He may have a Scottish granny. Then again he may not. No one really cares, just like no one really cares about Dan's opinions on matters Scottish. He may have gone to Inverness on holiday once, if that's a help. He's only on the committee to make sure the SNP are outnumbered.

Maggie Throup is the Tory MP for Erewash, which I always thought was one of the kingdoms of Middle Earth, but apparently it's in Derbyshire. Maggie may or may not be an elf, but we can be sure that her contribution to Scottish debates won't be magic. Maggie was chosen for the committee because Derbyshire was the most southern point that the Jacobite rebels reached in the 18th century, and Davie Cameron is hoping that Maggie will turn around the Caledonian hordes with her magic wand. Her Wikipedia page says "Maggie Throup is the Conservative MP for Erewash" and practically nothing else, that's how great her dedication to Scottish matters is.

So these are the people that Westminster has chosen to have a majority on the only committee that will scrutinise legislation and ensure that it's in tune with the desires and needs of the Scottish electorate. They'd probably have stood a better chance of finding people more representative of Scottish public opinion if they'd made a random selection of backing singers from Croatian entries to Eurovision from the past decade. But then representing Scotland isn't what a Westminster Scottish Affairs Committee is all about. It's about ensuring that Scotland's affairs are dictated by Westminster, and about making sure that we don't get any notions that we get a choice in the matter.

Can we have another independence referendum now please? This isn't funny anymore.

**Update:** It's worse than I thought. There's 11 of them, not 10. And there's the same number of Tories as SNP MPs. The extra Tory is John Stevenson who represents Carlisle. Carlisle used to be a part of Scotland until the 11th century. It's even got a Gaelic name *Cathair-Luail*, but we really don't want it back. They vote for folk like John, who was educated in Aiberdeen but had to go to Carlisle in order to find people who'd vote for him and his brand of old fashioned homophobia. John doesn't like the idea that gay people can get married, but then most gay people - and a hell of a lot of straight people - don't really like the idea of John either. So there's some balance.

## The Hangover from a 300 Year Binge

*4 July 2015*

Oh god. Ma heid. Ma second class representation in the Westminster Parliament. Is there such as thing as syrup of figs for a blocked devolution settlement? Being Scottish in the UK feels like waking up with a 300 year hangover. The groggy recollection that you did some really bad things with India and Africa, the slowly dawning realisation that you've got bugger all to show for it, and the growing awareness that you have, in fact, been taken for a complete mug. The things you've done and the place you're in now are not who you really are. There's an immense mismatch between how you see yourself and how your drinking companion sees you, the one who's been poncing off you for years and filling your head with crap. And you believed it. It's cringe-making.

Scotland sees itself as a country. Because that's what we are. Instinctively we compare ourselves with other small countries like Denmark or Finland. Scottish people do this even without thinking about it. It is ingrained deep within us that we are a country and a nation. And the consequence of being a country and a nation is that it makes us a unit of sovereignty. Even many people who voted No last year share this view. It's for Scotland and her people to decide whether we remain within the UK or not. We're a unit of sovereignty and have the sovereign right to decide our own future.

The Westminster Parliament doesn't see us like we see ourselves. That's why Westminster's refusal to take on board the wishes of the vast majority of Scotland's elected representatives feels like a slap in the face. We already knew we were facing rejection, but rejection still hurts even when you were expecting it. Westminster's braying Tories and ignorant Labourites don't look upon Scotland see a sovereign nation. They look to the north and they see us as a problematic region which formerly returned a block of Labour MPs as reliably as an alkie turns to a Buckie bottle.

Scotland had a minor supporting role in the Westminster chorus, but now we're singing a different tune. Scotland has sobered up, we're looking at the empty glass and we're just not parliamentary fun anymore. We can no longer be relied upon, no longer be trusted to play our part in the game. We're Westminster's alcoholic pal who has given up the drink and discovered politics instead, and that means we're boring and tedious and need to be side lined and silenced. Scotland has discovered that the stories of a union of equals, a partnership, they were only ever that. Stories to tell over an opened bottle to a hauf cut drunk who could be relied upon not to remember.

Tim Farron has grasped this. He wants to silence the sobered up Scotland. Tim wants to become leader of what's left of the Lib Dems, which is a bit like wanting to lead the 7th Cavalry after the Battle of the Little Big Horn only with Alistair Carmichael's refusal to resign as a last stand. Tim's got a well thought out Scottish policy. It's "SNP bad, SNP very bad, SNP practically Nazis but I'm not actually going to say the N word because then my poverty of ideas becomes painfully apparent even to the Scottish media."

On Saturday Tim gave an interview to the Herald in which he said that nationalism can be progressive when it's getting crapped on from a great height, but when it's ascendant it's always borderline fascist - or just plain outright let's go and invade Poland. Tim wants to ensure that Scottish nationalism remains a progressive force by continuing to crap on it from a great height. So he's doing us all a favour really. He's joined in his favour doing by Labour and the Tories, none of whom have the slightest idea of what to do about this newly conscious Scotland except repeat the mantra of SNP bad and hope that in despair we will return to the bottle.

It's not going to happen. We woke up. We briefly glimpsed a vision of what could be. We learned what hope felt like. We discovered that things don't have to be the way that our masters in the corridors of power in London want them to be. We discovered the radical notion that a country could be run for the benefit of its citizens and not for the benefit of banks and big business. It's a sweeter taste than wine.

The Tim Farrons and the Davie Camerons and the faceless drone devoid of personality who will inherit the Labour mantle are the mental giants into whose hands Scotland's No voters surrendered the country on 18th

September last year. These are the people whose meanness of spirit and narrowness of vision constrict our future like a vice. They offer us nothing but a return to the Buckie and baksheesh of Westminster, their brain death and corruption.

Now I know it's not fashionable to criticise No voters, on account of the fact that we need to persuade them to vote Yes if Scotland is ever to get away from the likes of Tim and live in a universe which involves joined up thinking and grown up politics. However, I can't help but tell the No voters I know that all this rubbish, these insults, this disdain and contempt, it is all because you were suckered, because you were taken in, because you lost your nerve, because you were tricked into drinking a deep draught from the Buckie bottle. That's why we suffer the cuts and wounds of a Tory government. That's why anyone has to take Michael Gove seriously instead of entering him in Britain's Got Talent as a goldfish lookalike. I'm sorry about this, but that's the bottom line. No voters made a call in September based upon lies and deceit, and now we all have to suffer the consequences. But we can all feel better about ourselves by blaming the Daily Record for not caring about the difference between Labour lies and news.

It's not too late to redeem things. There is still hope of change. We can still dream of a better life and a better country. It's coming, there's still time to say yes to hope.

## The Scottish Play

*6 July 2015*

You can say pretty much what you like in the British media, especially about Scotland. You can publish screaming headlines that tell outright lies about public figures, especially if they support Scottish independence. You can spread falsehoods and by simple repetition make them into truths, like the lie that Scotland would be automatically excluded from the EU if it became independent. You can invent fictions like Gordie Broon's vow and turn them into game changing events. And you can get away with it. Or in the case of the Record and Gordie's vow, or Reporting Scotland and its unending diet of kittens fitba and SNP bad, you can even get an award for it. It's the programme of the Scottish play.

It seems that the very worst that's going to happen when a newspaper doesn't do its job is that it gets a slap on the wrist and has to publish a retraction, buried away on an inside page where it will remain unseen and unexamined. It's like being told you must atone for lying by going deep into a dark and trackless forest and whispering the truth to a tree - before taking a chainsaw to it and turning it into paper on which you print the latest shocking news of Kim Kardashian's nail job from hell, or something about the fitba.

This is exactly what has happened with the report of the memo published by the Telegraph which wrongly alleged that Nicola Sturgeon told the French ambassador that she wanted the Tories to win the election. The Independent Press Standards Organisation upheld a complaint against the paper's reporting of the Frenchgate memo, and told the Telegraph to inscribe an apology on a leaf on a poison vine, parasitising a tree deep within the Amazonian rain forest where not even Sting is going to find it and do a benefit concert to publicise its plight. And with that, Scotland's lip was plugged, but not in a shaman kind of way. Although it is fair to say that much of the UK coverage of Scottish affairs reads like it was written after the reporters had ingested some of the more psychoactive South American shrubbery.

Having been told by IPSO that its report was wrong and needed to be corrected, the Telegraph obliged, and printed a five line comment on an inside page by way of compensation for its thousands of words of front page lies, its photo spreads and the acreage of commentary and news their story provoked elsewhere in the fair and balanced media with the Amazonian trippy plants up its nose. Because that's fair and balanced.

So we are now in the lamentable position where most of the mainstream media and a large part of the Scottish public hold one another in open contempt. The public regard the media with suspicion and won't take anything it says at face value. And the media's representatives regard the public with disdain. You can't maintain a democracy under such circumstances. How can the media scrutinise and bring to heel powerful vested interests when the public believes that the media is a powerful vested interest that is beyond scrutiny and beyond control?

It's because of the incompetence of the media that we get a Tory government which, when asked to list what it considered English only legislation, included the Scotland Bill. Before some readers get worked up into an outrage at how Scotland's devolution is apparently considered an English only matter by our Tory masters, the inclusion of the Scotland Bill on the list was clearly a mistake, or a wind up. So instead feel free to get worked up into an outrage at the fact we are governed by morons who are not held to account by a media inhabited with venal idiots.

If we had a media which properly scrutinised the UK government on Scotland's issues, eejit Tory politicians might think twice before releasing a list of English only legislation to the media, when that list contains the Scotland Bill. Clearly no one had bothered to read the list. Conveniently this provides us with an answer to the question of just how much scrutiny our political masters are being subjected to. It's none at all. Scotland is defenceless before the most right wing Tory government ever.

But our government is not merely viciously right wing, and entirely bereft of a democratic mandate in Scotland, it's so shambolic that it makes Wullie Rennie look like he's a yoga master with the power to retract his own genitals into his body at will leaving nothing but an empty scrotum. Which may explain the habitual look on his face. But that's the sort of dickless bawbags we've got for a government. And by and large the UK media does not seem particularly concerned by this state of affairs. Worse than that, most of them are egging them on to punish us even more.

We've become used to the charade now when the Westminster Parliament debates Scottish affairs. There's an empty chamber in the Commons, only the SNP and a handful of other MPs turn up. There's a gobsmackingly insane point of order from Jacob Rees Mogg. An irrelevant intervention from a Labour MP who thinks the debate is really about something else entirely. Then a vote is called, Scotland's MPs troop into the division to vote one way, and they're instantly outnumbered by hordes of Tories and Labour MPs who appear out of nowhere and vote them down without bothering to sit through Jacob Ree Mogg - although to be fair that last bit is entirely reasonable. Unless you have think a refugee from Jeeves and Wooster is of cutting edge relevance to modern Scotland there is no point to Jacob at all. There are primary school nativity plays which are considerably closer to an accurate depiction of reality than the House of Commons debating Scotland. The entire affair is a pointless ritual, the semblance of democracy but none of the substance, and if we had a media that actually did its job they'd be screaming that fact from the rooftops.

We're only at the start of Act 1 Scene 1 in the Westminster Scottish play, and Scotland is bored already. How much more of this can we take before we vote with our feet?

## Tory Budget Blues

*8 July 2015*

**W**hen I was a wean, budget day was about the price of beer and ciggies. It was about how much a gallon of petrol was going to cost. Now it's about how little poor people are going to have to eat. It's about how many young people whose family lives have broken down are going to find themselves sleeping in doorways. It's about how many disabled people and their carers are going to be trapped without support or respite. It's about how many low paid workers are going to find themselves trapped in a cycle of debt without job security. And it's about tax concessions for those who are already well off, the braying middle classes whose sense of entitlement grows ever greater. Budget day is about the rich getting richer on the broken backs of the poor. It's about a fractured society ruled by those who know the price of everything but the value of nothing.

There's been a sleight of hand rebranding of the minimum wage as a living wage which isn't a living wage, but a massive slashing of tax credits for low paid workers. The poorest paid aren't going to be any better off as a result of this budget. As usual, the ones who will benefit will be those who are already better off. It will be those who expect to inherit a million quid from the bank of mum and dad. It will be those on higher than average wages who've been taken out of the highest tax brackets. The tired grey faces on the bus will stay tired and grey, worried about job insecurity, worried about paying the rent, worried about putting food on the table, worried about paying for clothes for the weans. But Jocasta and Farquhar will be jetting off to the Seychelles, so that's OK then.

So some days, you find that your natural reservoirs of patience and tolerance have run dry. Like when you see Labour people on Twitter complain about evil Tory budgets which slash the support for the poor and marginalised, give tax breaks to the better off and increase spending on the military. The word hypocrite was invented for people like that.

You can't help but tell yourself that this is what they voted for after all. We had a chance to escape from this fate, but when the voters of Scotland were asked to think about the future of their country, Labour told them to think about the price of their car insurance and their holidays to Portugal. They scared them with threats to their pensions, they assured them that the NHS was safe. They lied, they threatened. And worst of all they stood shoulder to shoulder with those Tories they now condemn, and they did this in the full knowledge that Scotland might one day find itself prostrate and defenceless against the axe wielding maniacs of the neo conservative right. They lied and bullied so that Scotland would remain defenceless and incapable of deciding a different path for itself. They insisted that living with the very real threat of Tory rule was better than independence. Then they complain that we are subject to the fate that they wanted for us, and moan that some people call them rude names on the Internet. Well Labour, you got what you fought for. Dry your crocodile tears and suck it up.

So their protestations now against the unfairness and mendacity of Tory budgets ring as hollow as Ian Murray's head. They've not got a leg to stand on, just like the poor who have had their support cut off at the knees thanks to the Tories' benefits cuts. And all there is left to say to the bankrupt ideologues of Labour is - what the hell did you expect, fools? This is the consequence of what you fought for. You did this. You brought this on yourself, and you brought it on the rest of is. It's only a pity that moral indignation doesn't bring much of a comfort. It's the only wealth we've got left.

Neither do Labour and its media friends have any right to complain that that Scotland's single Tory MP has been able to reject every single amendment to the Scotland Bill. One MP gets to overrule 58. As far as Scotland is concerned, it's like the General Election didn't happen. The Conservatives are stuck in a watered down version of the Smith Commission time warp, and refuse to recognise that Scotland's vote in May was a vote for greater powers for Scotland, that it was a vote to reject the inadequacies of the Smith Commission.

None of this matters. The Tories have a majority, and Labour and its media pals enabled it. They worked to ensure that Scotland remained in a place of powerlessness. Of course what evil Tories do is the fault of the evil Tories, but it's also the fault of the Labour party. It's the fault of the Daily Record, it's the fault of the Lib Dems. They campaigned for Scotland to leave its arse exposed to the Tory air, they can't complain now that it's getting kicked.

This budget comes just a day after Kezia Dugdale, the candidate for leader of the Labour party in Scotland, said that the party had done too much for the vulnerable, and needed to concentrate more on those who have holidays in Portugal and complain about their car insurance. So we know what their priorities are going to be. Not fairness, not justice, not social inclusion, not democracy for Scotland.

So this is where we are. A nation that's not allowed to act like a nation, trussed up on the table of a Tory banquet where we are the meal not a dinner guest, and we're served up to someone else. The Conservative knives dig into our flesh and cut off slices for the bankers and the rich. And Labour chose this fate for us. They worked to make it happen. They don't get to complain about it, and they certainly don't get to lead the struggle against it. Scotland's independence supporters are the new labour movement, not that sorry excuse of a self-serving party.

This is where we are, but it's not where we need to remain. Every day, the appeal of independence grows ever more attractive. Every day, the hypothetical risks of self-determination shrink before the brutal realities of life in the UK.

Here were are in the dark days, the bleak times, the depths of winter, suffering the Tory budget blues. But the light of a Scottish spring is coming yet.

## Stalling the EVEL Minion Monkeys

*10 July 2015*

The evil Tories have had to make an evil delay to their evil EVEL plans. Not because they've suddenly realised that it's evil to make major constitutional changes through the back door of a procedural amendment which turns the people of Scotland into second class citizens with second class political representation in the Better Together on the Back Seat Parliament, they're actually pretty mellow with that entire concept. In fact, ensuring that Scotland is marginalised, castrated, and side lined is pretty much what the Conservative Scottish policy consists of. This has been the case since the days of Maggie Thatcher, and nothing much has changed ever since. The Tories don't do democracy as far as Scotland is concerned. Scotland is a problem, not a partner nation in a union.

But then common morality and basic decency doesn't rank high in the Conservative agenda either. These are after all people who think it's perfectly acceptable to make a raped woman prove to a faceless pen-pusher in the job centre that she's been raped so that she can get benefits for a child who is a product of that rape. This is despite the fact that most rapes go unreported, that women who have been raped find it immensely difficult to talk about the hell that they have gone through, or that an untrained benefits clerk who has been told to refuse payments to as many claimants as possible has zero experience in dealing with the trauma faced by a rape survivor and moreover has an incentive for not believing her. Given that the Tories have plumbed those depths of moral decreptitude and yet think it's perfectly acceptable, screwing over Scotland's constitutional rights is but a minor infringement in the cosmic ledger of good and evil. These are some pretty sick puppies we're talking about here. And all the sicker for not realising just how sick in the heads they are.

So it's not for any high minded reasons that EVEL has been delayed. Oh no, it's for the purely practical reason that Cameron's little bunch of minion monkeys don't think they'll get sufficient support from their own side to turn Scotland into a second class part of the UK. Some Tory monkeys have been throwing poo at the idea. And this is not because these Tory opponents have a moral stance against turning the screws on Scotland, the Tory opponents are quite happy to screw Scotland over because they read the Daily Mail too. It's just that besides wanting to screw over Scotland, they also fetishise the Westminster Parliament and don't want to make any changes to its arcane procedures at all. Not even changing the menu in the café. Some people really do believe that a Victorian pretendy idea of a mediaeval parliament really is the best way to run a 21st century country.

So the Government has retired to make a few tweaks to its EVEL proposals, and doubtless to make a few private inducements to some of the more reluctant members of the Tory party. You know, like holding up a wriggling white weasel and telling the MP concerned that it's just waiting to be killed, skinned and turned into ermine robes. And all they need to agree to is to kill and skin Scotland's chances of ever participating in this misbegotten Union as an equal partner. This is how constitutional amendments get made in a state without a written constitution. There is no principle involved, just what the governing party in Parliament can get away with. And Labour and the Lib Dems campaigned for us to remain a part of this system, so cheers for that.

EVEL, like psychotic killing robots, will be back, although unlike Arnie Swartzenegger it won't have morphed into the good guy in the sequel, although - like most sequels - it will be even more tedious and predictable the next time round.

Meanwhile Kezia Dugdale, candidate branch office manager of the Labour party in Scotland, has called on the SNP to set out how they propose to defend Scotland from the evil Tories. Kezia clearly has been far too busy screaming SNP bad to listen to anything that the SNP have ever had to say, because the SNP were not, as everyone except Kezia recalls, the ones who wanted us to remain a part of a state where we'd get Conservative governments despite the fact that the party only has one MP in Scotland.

Perhaps Kezia inhabits a universe in which the SNP spent the referendum campaign trying to persuade Scotland that we were Better Together with the risk of a majority Tory government that voters in Scotland didn't elect, but it's certainly not the one the rest of us inhabit. Back in this universe, as opposed to the Labour press release universe, the SNP propose to defend Scotland from Tory governments that we didn't elect by ensuring that we never ever have a Tory government, or indeed any government, that we didn't elect ever again. We can do that if we have independence, because if you are an independent nation then you get the government that people vote for at elections, and not the one a neighbouring country has voted for. This is a policy position which benefits from impeccable logic, something that you can never accuse the Labour party in Scotland of possessing.

Kezia wants the SNP to say how they will use the powers of Holyrood to mitigate the damage the Tories are wreaking, when it was Kezia's party which bent over backwards to ensure that Holyrood doesn't have any substantive powers to protect Scotland from Tory economic policy. It's like giving someone a 20 year old computer with a knackered floppy disk drive, and then getting annoyed with them because they keep getting beat at Grand Theft Auto. Labour deliberately made sure that Holyrood had unusable tax powers precisely so they could moan about them not being used. It was all a part of the con trick that the party has played on the people of Scotland for decades, only now they're complaining because we've seen through them.

## What Is the Point of You?

*12 July 2015*

Jesus wept, Keir Hardie spun in his grave, the ghost of Aneurin Bevin howled in impotent rage at the vacuity of the press release, the spirits of the Jarrow marchers sat down and wept, and millions of former supporters raised their eyebrows to the skies and sighed at the Labour party - what is the bloody point of you? And the only answer is the meaningless self-serving waffle of a party that's lost its way, a party that couldn't even find a moral compass if it was lodged up its own arse.

There is no point to Labour, none at all. No meaning. No purpose. No bloody sense. All there is is the cold hearted triangulation of a spin doctor who's never had to struggle against poverty or exclusion. Labour has announced that there's very little they're going to do to oppose as the Tories set fire to the social contract that Labour fought so hard to establish all those decades ago. The party is not going to oppose the cuts that the Tories are introducing to the benefits system, not going to oppose the loss of the principle that each mouth deserve to be fed. They've abandoned the principle of to each according to their need. Labour not only supports the final cutting through of the social safety net, they're helping the Tories with the scissors. Spin and snip as they cut their own tendons, and the party falls never to stand again.

What is the point of you Labour? Nothing, nothing but to make us weep and rage at your wilful impotence, to scream silently in the vacuum of your lost soul. The hopes of our grandparents betrayed, their memories traduced. What is the point of you?

When you lose your principles, you lose your soul. A week is a long time in politics, and in fifty years you can lose your soul and turn into a zombie, the living husk of a political party, going through the motions but without any sense of purpose. Labour is the vampire party, sucking on the aspirations and hopes of working class people, existing for nothing but the perpetuation of its cadre of politicians. The lesson this teaches us is that one Labour MP, one Labour MSP, one Labour councillor, is one too many. We must do to them what we did to the Tories - consign them to the wilderness of political untouchability.

The Tories pretend to govern in the interests of the whole country, and Labour pretend to oppose them. The little people are expected to continue with a charade that wouldn't be out of place in a dystopian novel, living a harsh reality caught between two falsehoods.

Labour in Scotland demand that the SNP set out they're going to protect Scotland's poor from the Tory cuts, while UK Labour refuse to oppose them. This is clearly what they meant during the independence referendum when they claimed that being part of the UK produced the best of both worlds. Labour gets to have its austerity cake across the UK as a whole, and still gets its SNP bad headlines in the Daily Record. The Tory media propagates the lie that the financial crisis was the fault of the poor, and Labour doesn't have the balls to stand up and call a lie a lie. It meekly goes along with it in the hope of sooking up to the middle class voters in Tory swing seats. Labour is happy with the notion of making those who rely on benefits and those on low wages foot the bill for the financial disaster that Labour and the Tories allowed to happen by turning a blind eye to the excesses of the banks. The lost themselves in the pursuit of power and money.

So this is the redistribution that Gordie Broon spoke of, the redistribution of wealth from the poor to the rich. Pooling and sharing means the poor pool so that the rich can share. And Labour is just fine with all of this, because even the most mousy mealy mouthed protest will attract the wrath of press barons that Labour never had the balls to hold in check. Labour created the means of its own destruction, and acquiesces in it meekly. Well they can destroy themselves, but we're damned if they take us with them.

The party has lost the ability to distinguish between right and wrong, to tell the difference between good and evil. When you can't even bring yourself to oppose such an obvious obscenity as insisting that a woman who has a third child as a result of rape must prove that rape to a faceless official in the Job Centre who has an incentive for not believing her, then all is lost.

Labour's excuse is that it would be wrong of them to tell voters that they were wrong to vote for a party that does wrong. When Labour is too afraid to defend what's right in case it stops them getting the votes of those who support wrong - what's the point of you then Labour? If the only way to become the government is to become the Tories, then there is no need to bother with a Labour party at all. We've already got evil Tories, we don't require any more of them. We have them in abundance already.

And this, Labour, this is why we no longer tolerate you amongst us, why you can no longer participate in our struggles. You are dead to us because you're dead to yourselves. The annihilation you experienced in May was only the beginning, by the time we've finished with you you will be a footnote in history. We are the opposition to the Tories, not you.

So to the last few remnants of that battered party - if you have a shred of dignity left, if you still value the hopes and aspirations of the working classes above the pursuit of power for power's sake, then leave Labour, take to the lifeboats, join the SNP, the Greens, the SSP, and help us build a better Scotland. Help us to push the doors of opportunity open, or decline into a sub-Tory irrelevance, bereft of principle, meaning or morality. There is a better way, a way out of this nightmare. It's called independence. And now it's clearer than it ever was that it's the only escape.

## It's Been a Good Week

*14 July 2015*

I t's been a good week. OK, we still have the slimiest evillest Tory government since slimy evil first crawled out of the primordial slimy evil soup - which by a strange coincidence was also the stuff they used to serve up in the school canteen when I was a wean. But apart from that, it's been a good week.

It's been a good week because today, the 14th of July, is Bastille Day. This is the day that the peasants of France finally had enough of their ruling classes, and rose up and deposed them. Meanwhile King Louis XVI wrote in his diary for that day *rien* - nothing. You'd think that after 230 years the ruling elites of Europe, and the UK, might have learned by now of the dangers of being so out of touch with public opinion. But apparently not. *Plus ça change, plus c'est la même chose.*

It's been a good week because the New Horizons probe flew all the way through the solar system to the frozen depths of Pluto, where it got a much warmer welcome than a benefits claimant in a Tory budget and confirmed that even from that distance George Osborne still looks like a slimy evil lying git far beyond any possible redemption.

It's been a good week because the Large Hadron Collider - which I keep mistyping as Large Hardon Collider because I can't get my mind out the gutter, although I'm sure that it's a sport played in some of the more specialist night clubs - has discovered a new subatomic particle. The pentaquark is mind bogglingly tiny, but it's still several orders of magnitude greater than Iain Duncan Smith's generosity.

It's been a good week because the sun has finally taken its tap aff and keeked out from behind its Scottish blanket of cloud and admitted that it's the middle of July. Although of course it won't last. The sun in Scotland is more skitterish than a fox in a room full of Tory MPs.

It's been a good week because I'm loved up, having met a friend in Boston that I've chatted with for years. Our eyes met, and let's just say that there was a Grangemouth's worth of chemistry. The dug's got himself a new American boyfriend. Unlike the sun in a Scottish summer, that's a warmth that will last. He does read this blog occasionally, and says things like, "What does tap aff mean?" So I demonstrate, and that's quite enough information.

And it's a good week because Scotland's 56 opposition MPs - the Labour one and Lib Dem one don't count because they're bugger all use for anything - actually managed to get the slimy evil Tories to crawl back into their primordial evil soup while complaining about the SNP being opportunistic. Which is a bit like Dracula complaining about blood banks.

Davie Cameron is upset because Scotland's MPs shouldn't be allowed to overrule England's MPs, this comes after the single Scottish Tory overruled every single amendment to the Scotland Bill made by the 58 non-Tory Scottish MPs. Paddington Mundell doesn't have 59 votes all by himself, but he does count on the support of a whole load of English MPs who will vote down what Scotland wants. Cameron doesn't do irony where Scotland is concerned, or indeed fairness or democracy.

As a result of the SNP's decision to intervene on the fox hunting issue, the Tories have been forced to withdraw the motion to repeal the hunting ban because they were unsure that they would be able to get it to pass. It's quite possible that it will not return in this Parliament, or ever, and English foxes have the SNP to thank for it. They're now free to return to raiding rubbish bins like reporters for the Daily Mail. Although if it had been a vote on whether to allow Daily Mail reporters to be hunted down with dogs, it's highly probable that the SNP would have voted in favour. I know I would have.

But the real reason for the intervention was to remind Cameron and his minions that they do not always enjoy the crushing majority that they have when they use the weight of their 300 English MPs to overrule 58 Scottish ones. And if they want to play that game, then they ought to be prepared for others to play it back at them. And to play it with considerably more style and panache.

Then it's been a good week because there was an opinion poll. There haven't been many Scottish opinion polls since the election, and this latest one asked about voting intentions in next year's Holyrood vote. This is important, as it's vital we secure a clear majority of pro-independence MSPs if there is to be a chance of a new independence referendum. And the poll showed that the SNP and the Greens are likely to enjoy a crushing majority in Holyrood.

The poll also showed that 60% of Scots want another independence referendum within 10 years, although most would still vote no - but the good news is that less than a year after the indyref the 55% are now only the 52%, and if we keep up this rate of attrition they'll be well under 40% by the time there's an indyref2. You see that light on the horizon? That's an independent Scotland coming that is.

That the Union is on the wrong side of history was shown by the maiden speech of Scotland's youngest MP, the 20 year old Mhairi Black. In a stupendous speech she was witty and gracious - and begged Labour to join with the SNP in being a constructive opposition to the Tories. The fact that the voice of Scotland's youth and Scotland's future had to plead with Labour to get it to do what it was supposed to be doing all along tells you all you need to know about the likely future of Labour and the Union. Them and the Tories are the Louis XVI of the 21st century - although they're only in for a metaphorical beheading.

So we listened to the articulate and passionate words of an intelligent young working class Scottish woman, telling them what it is in the House of Commons. And you know that the future is good.

It's been a good week.

## BBC Cringe: the Norma Desmond of Broadcasters

*16 July 2015*

Earlier this week, the youngest Scottish MP ever gave her maiden speech in the Chamber of the House of Commons. You'd think that a 20 year old working class Scottish woman from Paisley might be intimidated by an institution which is so far up its own arse that the crap comes out the other end, but not Mhairi Black. Since deposing one of the spoiled princes of the Labour party from the seat, Mhairi has been subjected to a barrage of insults and abuse from the UK media. She has been patronised and demeaned by middle aged middle class privileged men who are affronted that someone like Mhairi dares not just to step onto their territory, but to own it. And that's precisely what Mhairi did in the House of Commons with her maiden speech.

The speech was perfectly judged, contained the right balance of humour and gravity, it was emotional and emotive, but at the same time logical and rational. She spoke movingly and with great passion about the evil wrought on working class communities by an ideologically driven Conservative government. She made it personal and illustrated the destructive effect that Tory benefit rules have on ordinary people. There but for the grace of god could go any one of us. She pleaded with the

Labour party not to acquiesce and surrender to Tory policies but to join with the SNP in actively opposing the Government and to challenge it. And you know that Labour have fallen pretty low when it takes a 20 year old to plead with them to oppose the Tories. Some Labour MPs had the good grace to look shamed and a bit embarrassed, although Ian Murray wasn't amongst them.

Even cynical auld gits like me were moved by Mhairi's words. It would have been a remarkable and newsworthy speech irrespective of whose mouth it had issued from. And it issued from the mouth of a young working class Scottish woman. Mhairi did herself proud, she did her constituency proud, she did Scotland proud, she did democracy proud. Mhairi showed that Scotland's future is safe and secure, because she's the voice of the next generation. You couldn't help but feel as you watched her that you were watching the president of a future Scottish republic.

So how did the Scottish state broadcaster choose to report on this marvellous affirmation of Scottish democracy, this immense credit to the youth of our country? It told us that the SNP had been slapped down by the deputy speaker for applauding Mhairi's speech. There was a clip of the deputy speaker instructing MPs that they could show approval by harrumphing like trained seals, but there wasn't a single line of Mhairi's own words. This is the news we pay for. This is the news that we have to pay a tax on. And now we know the difference between a state broadcaster and a public service.

According to the nearest thing that Scotland has to a public broadcaster, the only important thing about Mhairi Black's speech was that there was a mild breach of the antiquated and sclerotic protocol of the House of Commons as Mhairi's SNP colleagues showed their appreciation. Another belter of a maiden speech, from the wonderful Anne McLaughlin, the Sherpa Tenzing of Glasgow North East who climbed the mountain of the largest Labour majority in the country, and got to the top in style - that went entirely unreported. The message from BBC Scotland was clear - Scotland, you're a bit rubbish and you need to be slapped down and put in your place.

BBC Scotland's news department apparently operates on the default assumption that nothing good can possibly come of the SNP. Let's find someone who had to wait more than four hours in A&E and use it to attack the Scottish Government. Any mistake or oversight by a public body in Scotland becomes a generalised attack on Scottish self-government.

BBC Scotland should just quit pretending that it's a public service broadcaster, it's an arm of the British state. It's not BBC Scotland, it's BBC Cringe - and don't you Scots dare forget just how irrelevant and rubbish you are. It's not a public service, it's not remotely representative of the public it is supposed to service, it's the propaganda department of the British state. It's wall to wall crap about the Royal bloody family. I honestly don't give a crap about Willnkate and their gilded existence. Now here's a story about a cute kitten stuck up a tree that had to wait hours before the SNP's national fire service could come and rescue it. And now the fitba.

This is not to criticise the ordinary staff of BBC Scotland. They have families to feed just like anyone else, and they are not responsible for the Corporation's editorial policies which are set and controlled by London. I know for a fact that many amongst the ordinary staff of BBC Scotland support the proper devolution of BBC Scotland and yearn to make it into the proper Scottish public broadcaster that it was always supposed to be. Sadly, the chances of that happening are close to zero as the Corporation battens down the hatches in the face of a concerted attack from the Tory government. Screwing the Scots is one way in which the BBC management in London can demonstrate its loyalty and avoid cuts and axes in other areas which are more important to the London based elite which determines BBC policy.

The BBC in Scotland has long since lost its reputation for impartiality, however much it clings to the memory of its former glory. By its one sided handling of the referendum campaign, its relentless focus on SNP Bad, BBC Scotland has destroyed itself as a credible news organisation. It has now got to the point where BBC Scotland could highlight a major failure of the Scottish government and thousands of perfectly reasonable people will turn a deaf ear, because BBC Scotland has cried wolf many times too often. BBC Scotland is the Norma Desmond of news, it thinks that it's the news that's got small.

So what to do about it? I recently paid my TV licence for the year so it would be hypocritical for me to call on other people not to pay it and to take the risk of prosecution that I'm not facing myself. Although I have to say that it's unlikely that I'm going to renew my TV licence - I don't see why I should pay for propaganda. If the BBC wants to punt an ideologically driven message to me, they should be paying me for the privilege, I don't see why I should be paying them for royalist pro-union advertising.

But it's not enough just to withhold the TV licence, we need to decide what we want in place of BBC Cringe, and we need to decide how to go about getting it. We need the devolution of broadcasting now. The 56 SNP MPs in Westminster and the Scottish Government should highlight the issue at every opportunity - Scotland is the *only* self-governing country in the world which doesn't have its own public service broadcaster. So much for best of both worlds.

## The Party Which Ran Away

### 21 July 2015

Are there any principles left in the moral vacuity that has replaced the Labour party? Is there anything that can be said that will get through to the party's bankrupt leadership? Are there any barbs sharp enough to pierce the elephant's hide of complacency that surrounds Labour's sense of entitlement? On the showing up the party gave itself in the House of Commons on Monday night, the answer to all three questions is clearly no. Edward VIII had more principles than Labour do, that's how low Labour has sunk.

Just 48 Labour MPs had enough of a moral conscience remaining to vote against the Tories' swingeing and ideologically driven cuts to the benefits system. The rest are the St Augustines of political opposition - every night they get down on their knees to worship Mammon and pray that their god grants the strength to resist the Tories - but not yet. Let's be clear here, the it wasn't the poor, the disabled, or carers who caused the economic crisis. It wasn't the low paid who caused the national debt to soar. It was the fault of the banks and their unregulated casino, it was the fault of rich corporations and individuals who have systematically avoided paying their fair share. And it was the fault of the Tories and the

Labour party for allowing this sorry state of affairs to come to pass. And now as the Tories seek to punish the poor for the sins of the rich, Labour washes its hands in crocodile tears and says it does nothing for our own good. Labour dishonours our grandparents who founded that once great party. It traduces the memory of our struggles. Labour has betrayed the people it once stood for.

Only 48 Labour MPs remembered that they were elected to oppose. Scotland's sole Labour MP wasn't one of them. Did the residents of Edinburgh South elect him to oppose the Tories by acquiescing to them? That's what Ian seems to believe. More SNP MPs than Labour MPs voted against the Tories' vicious vindictiveness. Her Majesty's Opposition think their official title means that they can only oppose things that her maj and her Hitler saluting benefits claiming family of spongers would oppose.

If you're unemployed, Labour won't give you an income you can live on until you find work. If you're a carer, Labour doesn't care about you. If you're disabled, Labour wants you to stand on your own feet and will kick away your crutches. There was a time, a long time ago in a galaxy far far away, that Labour was the party that defended those who didn't have the resources to defend themselves. Now it's the party of the Death Star and the benefits sanction. It's the party of the shallow, the materialists, the selfish. Labour is only the party of No when No means telling Scotland it can't govern itself.

Only a fifth of Labour's MPs have a vestigial remnant of a moral purpose, have a memory of what their party once stood for. Only a tiny minority of Labour MPs could look Mary Barbour in the eye. Only a tiny minority of Labour MPs can still claim to be the heirs to the Red Clydesiders. Labour wants to be the party for people who want a second holiday to Portugal and riding lessons for the teenage daughter. Labour wants to be the Tory party. That means that the malaise that Labour suffers from is worse than penis envy, they suffer from arsehole envy.

The best you can say about the rest of the Labour party is that at least some of the party's MPs had the decency to turn up and abstain in person and stare their non-vote in its metaphorical blind eye. There are invertebrates with more of a spine, snakes with more legs to stand on. In the modern Labour party, it's a rebel MP who is the one to vote against Tory benefits cuts. A rebel MP, think on that. That's what happens when you try to run a country and formulate policy based on what focus groups in Croydon tell you.

You expect this sort of thing from Tories. Tories are callous and insensitive, however well preened the hairdos of their press apologists. The Tories kill the poor while Labour looks the other way, and tries to claim that looking the other way is a principled stance. The principle being - I'm going to walk past this mugging in the street without doing anything in solidarity with people who haven't been mugged. Someone needs to stand up for the non-mugging non-victims.

Ah but, say the Labour apologists, we'd have lost the vote anyway so it makes no difference. But that's not true, it would have made no difference to the outcome of the vote, but it would have made a hell of a difference to the tattered reputation of a pathetic excuse for a party. People might just actually have thought that Labour had some balls, and not the Tory budgeting Ed kind. People might have realised that Labour still stood for something. But now they know that Labour stands for nothing except a hauf-airsed petty fogging power grab, and when that fails they cower under a rock like the moral cowards they are. Labour is a party that no longer sings about keeping the red flag flying, the only flag they fly is a white one. They won't oppose anything if it risks resulting in a bad headline in the Daily Mail.

308 Tories voted in favour. 128 MPs opposed, the SNP, Plaid, the 48 Labour MPs with a conscience. 308 minus 128 is 180, and more than 180 Labour MPs abstained. Oh but because of pairing we'd still have lost, the Labour apologists bleat. Excuses about the cosy gentleman's pairing arrangement cut no ice when you're starving out on the streets in a bitterly cold winter. It's not the job of Labour to enter into cosy arrangements with the Tories, it's their job to make life difficult for them. But Labour don't want to do that if the Daily Telegraph objects. That's what makes Labour unfit for purpose.

Labour's spinelessness is why we didn't vote for them in Scotland - on this showing we'll never vote for them again. Labour recovery? Even BBC Scotland can't even start dreaming of that until there's a glimmer of hope that Labour might just do its bloody job. But we don't need Labour to oppose the Tories any more - we have the SNP and the Greens for that, and that's why Labour is going the way of the Union. The demise of Labour is the demise of the UK.

## Captain Caveman and the Shock of the New

*23 July 2015*

Labour's hierarchy, the careerists and the SPADs, the spin doctors and the politics grads, are in full scale panic mode this week. Headless chickens have been known to run around more calmly and with a greater sense of purpose. The cliques in charge of the Labour party these past 20 years have suddenly discovered that their corpse like grasp on the party is rotting away and the token leftie might actually win the election.

Curse this democracy and one member one vote business. Having changed the voting system to reduce the power of the unions, the Labour leadership has now made the shocking realisation that some Labour members actually believe in all that stuff about socialism and fairness and redistribution of wealth and holding the banks and the corporations to account for the financial crisis they've caused, instead of blaming the poor and the marginalised. The road to hell is paved with self-serving intentions and right wing machinations.

According to a Yougov poll, Jeremy Corbyn is well ahead in an election he wasn't supposed to win. He wasn't even supposed to make any significant impression in the leadership contest. He was supposed to come in a poor fourth, trailing behind Liz Kendall and her Blairite nostrums. He was there as socialist window dressing, a red sop to the membership, a little dash of red colourant to remind Labour of its roots. Jeremy's real role in the election contest, according to the bland plastic people who make up the rest of the field, was to say left wing things that they could reject so they could appear sensible and middle of the road. He was there so that none of them would have to look left wing. Jeremy's job was to give Liz, Andy, and Yvette someone to point a finger at and say socialism bad, so they'd get a marginally more sympathetic write up in an unsympathetic press.

But that's not what's happening. For those of us in Scotland this is popcorn time, as we sit back and watch the Westminster Labour party implode under the weight of its own self-delusion just as we watched its Scottish branch office do over the course of the past year. But the real worry is that whereas Labour in Scotland collapsed under the crushing weight of the SNP and the Greens and SSP and the well-articulated aspirations of a highly politicised populace who knew what they wanted and knew how to vote in order to get it, Labour in England implodes into a vacuum. There's nothing else left in the English body politic except the heartlessness of the Tories and the vultures of UKIP.

If Labour in England collapses, there's nothing to replace them. The SNP are going to have to do the job of the opposition in England too - is that what Better Together meant by Scotland punching above its weight as a part of the UK? Probably not.

The problem for Labour is that none of the four leadership contenders is a convincing leader, and if UK wide opinion polls are anything to go by, none are heading for 10 Downing Street at the next UK General Election. Labour looks set for a period in the wilderness while it rediscovers its soul and its purpose. So the question is will it find that soul and purpose under the management of the same plastic identikit politicians who brought it to this sorry pass, or will it find it with a leader who is likely to prove as unelectable as Michael Foot, but who will actively oppose the Tories and give the shattered party a sense of purpose again.

Meanwhile in Scotland we're faced with a different set of questions. With a Labour party that's not going to be re-electable in 2020, we have the very real and very scary prospect of George Osborne or Boris Johnson as the next UK Prime Minister - assuming that Cameron stands down before the next election as he has previously hinted. Is that the Union that No voters want to remain a part of, a dystopian hell of privileged elites and excluded masses, stretching ahead of us like a high speed railway that we are denied a ticket on. The UK train's destination is off a privatised cliff. We need to change track, we need to take control of our own destiny.

Meanwhile a demon from the past popped up to tell Labour where it's all going wrong. The war mongerer responsible, the soul-eater, the spirit crusher, the man who put morality through the blender of Iraq then waltzed off in a flurry of consultancies. Tony Blair gave a speech about the future of the party, and apparently didn't even charge for it this time. But then near bankrupt Labour doesn't have pockets as deep as Kazakhstani dictators. Tone created a Labour party in his own image and wants it to stay that way. Because soulless money grabbing war-mongerers are so progressive.

He also had a wee dig at the only effective political opposition left in the UK, the SNP. Tone said:

"When they talk about it being new politics, it is the oldest politics in the world. It's the politics of the first caveman council, when the caveman came out from a council where there were difficult decisions and pointed with his club across the forest and said: 'They're the problem, over there, that's the problem.' It's blaming someone else."

And this would be true, because the topic of the first caveman council was the fact that them over there across the forest were eating people's brains because they were unevolved apes with a sense of entitlement the size of a mammoth. We're still opposing the brain-eaters, Tone thinks the proper path is to eat brains too. Of course it's not "new" politics, because we saw how Tony defined new when he rebranded a social democratic party as New Labour. Then what he did was nothing new. Greed, avarice, wars and invasions are the oldest politics of all. Blair gave us the shock and horror of the new Labour. He can keep his new, we want no part of it.

## On the Highway to Indyref2

*26 July 2015*

Alicsammin is back in the news, not that he ever really left it. You may remember him from last year, while you, oh naive Caledonian person you, thought you were voting in an independence referendum, according to the UK media Scotland was voting in an Alicsammin's referendum. Alicsammin was, at least until the votes were counted, the only person in the entire UK who wanted independence. Or, according to the Daily Mail, to shamelessly rip the beating heart out of this great nation of ours out of hatred for all things English.

Anyway, Alicsammin has been annoying the UK media again by making the perfectly sensible and obvious point that another independence referendum is inevitable. This has led to an outbreak of ooohing and tutting in certain sections of the metrocommentariat, who are playing clips on an infinite loop of Alicsammin saying that the referendum was a once in a generation opportunity. They're doing this because they're still labouring under the misapprehension that it was Alicsammin's referendum.

But it wasn't, it was your referendum, it was my referendum, it was my maw's referendum, it was my late partner's referendum. It was your cousin's referendum, it was your pal's referendum. And no one asked us whether we thought it was only going to be a once in a generation deal. I don't recall the question on the ballot paper being - should Scotland be an independent country and should we never ever ask this question again in your lifetime?

The only question that is still open is the timing. We need another independence referendum. I want another independence referendum. And the only material change of circumstances that I'm interested in is the one that says we're going to win. We're not there yet, but support for independence has increased somewhat since the referendum. We need to build on that and increase it. The next time we have a referendum it needs to be a formality, the legal recognition of what will by then be the settled will of the Scottish people, the settled will to become independent.

Alicsammin said that there were already several reasons why another referendum is inevitable. There's the infamous vow for starters. At the fag end of the referendum campaign when the Union was a doubt we got promised devo to the max. Now Westminster says devo my arse. This super dooper near federalism home rule was supposed to have been overseen and supervised by the personal guarantee of Gordie Broon, who now makes the Invisible Man seem like a bit of an exhibitionist. Rumour has it he's pissed off to the USA. No one knows who he is over there so he can go to the shops and buy stuff without the risk of having his custom refused because no one has any change.

Despite voting for 56 SNP MPs who stood on a platform of yer Smith commish is pish, Scotland is still lumbered with the pathetically inadequate devo proposals that came out of that half hearted process. The only thing that we learned from the Smith Commission is that giving politicians the benefit of the doubt is always a mistake. It may take a few more years before that message percolates through to No voters, but slowly they're realising that they were had. A tipping point is in the offing.

Then there's the EU referendum, the Faragegasm of British politics. There's going to be a lot more of David Coburn in Scottish television studios, blazing away like a self-immolating bonfire of fart gas and blaming everything on immigrants and the SNP. But he's going to be a lonely voice as Coburn's appeal is very restricted, restricted to his own bathroom and a pile of Kleenex, and even the Kleenex doesn't want to be there. All by himself he will be enough to ensure a massive victory for staying in the EU from Scotland, no matter how intransigent Angela Merkel gets with small European countries who refuse to toe the austerity line.

However, in the rest of the UK, the immigrant bashing tendency is very much in the ascendant, and it's far from certain whether England will vote in favour to say in the EU, despite the Project Fear on Steroids which will be unleashed on the voters. We're in a different world now, where support from the mainstream media provokes suspicion and not trust. We may very well end up with a situation where Scotland votes to remain in the EU but the rest of the UK, or at least England, votes to leave.

That would turn the entire EU question on its head in the second indyref.

And finally there's the permausterity. Scotland didn't vote for that. We voted to grow our economy, we voted not to blame the poor and the low paid for the sins of the banks and the bosses. But we're getting Iain Duncan Smith making Cruella de Vile look like a patron of PETA, and George Osborne being touted as the next Prime Minister. The self-immolation of a Labour party that no longer has a clue what it's there for, what it's doing, or how it's supposed to get out of the hole it's dug for itself means that we're all facing being condemned to the Conservative con for another decade and a half. You want the Thatcher era all over again, only this time with no family silver in the form of nationalised industries to flog off? Well that's what you're getting, No voters. But there's still an escape route, and it's marked Indyref2.

In its report on the story, the BBC made the non-point that getting the UK government to agree to another referendum might prove to be very difficult indeed. Like any independence supporter thinks that we require their permission. The letter of the law may very well say that, but law is trumped by politics every time and if there is a large majority in the Scottish Parliament in favour of a referendum, and it is clear that a majority of the Scottish public wants independence, then we will have a referendum and we will have independence irrespective of what Westminster wants.

You want a legal principle for this? It's perfectly easy - it's the principle familiar to hundreds of thousands of

Scottish people when told that they can't do something, the principle of "Aye, that will be right." Scotland is still on the highway to independence, we've not reached the exit yet, but the journey is getting close to its end. We'll know that we're there when opinion polls show a consistent majority in favour of independence. And then we can have a party, and get down to some serious work.

## Scottish Democracy Is Not a Serving Suggestion

*28 July 2015*

Davie Cameron, the balloon faced Tory who enjoys the support of a single Scottish MP, has slapped down us little Scottish people who were labouring under the misapprehension that we lived in a democracy. He's done this in various ways. He's done it by giving us that nonentity striving for a purpose David Mundell, who in a normal universe would be a traffic warden, as Scotland's voice in the cabinet. He's done it by giving us a Scottish affairs committee in which Scottish MPs are outnumbers two to one by non-Scottish MPs. He's done it by refusing to recognise that the outcome of the General Election superseded the pathetic inadequacy of the Smith Commission and was a clear demand from Scotland for the substantial devolution that Davie and his pals promised us last year. But now he's also done it in another way.

This week Davie told Scotland that there's going to be no second independence referendum for 30 years. So, that's us telt then. Any time between now and 2044, it matters not a mundell if Scotland's voters overwhelmingly elect parties in favour of another referendum, parties who pledge in their manifestos to introduce a bill in Holyrood bringing forward a new referendum. For Davie and the Tories, Scottish democracy is merely a serving suggestion. You may select tender Scottish sovereignty in a rich creamy sauce with the roasted potatoes of representation, but what you're going to get is whatever mouldy instant noodles that Davie can dig out of the back of the cupboard where they keep the MI5 files on paedophile MPs.

But we shouldn't be disheartened. Westminster consented to the last referendum because they were convinced that the pro-independence cause would be lucky to get 25% of the vote, and the Union would win by such a crushing majority that the topic would be off the table for ever. As we all know, that's not what happened. Ha ha. The Union was saved by the skin of its teeth and only by making some very vague promises of sooper dooper extra powers for Scotland fronted by Saviour of the Union Gordie Broon. But the superpowers which Westminster never had any intention of delivering were always as imaginary as Gordie's superstatesman powers. The only people who ever believed in them were the editor of the Daily Record and BBC Scotland news.

The failure of the superpowers to arrive is stoking up increasing resentment in Scotland, only a small minority believe the oft repeated claim that the Union has delivered. But let's the honest here, this Union couldn't even deliver a pig in a poke. If David Cameron promised us a pig in a poke we'd end up with a packet of bacon flavour crisps that had long since gone as soggy as David Mundell. Meanwhile the saviour of the Union was so saved by his saving that he's now buggered off to the other side of the Atlantic as there wasn't a rock big enough in Scotland for him to hide under.

The reason that the Unionists are so keen to rule out a second referendum is because they are not at all certain that they're going to win it.

Westminster opposition to another independence referendum is likely to increase over time. The more likely it is that Scots are disposed to vote in favour of independence, the less likely it is that Westminster will willingly consent to a referendum taking place. For every percentage point that an independence majority increases over support for the Union, Project Fear 2.0 will ratchet up even more. We went into the last referendum campaign with a clear majority in favour of saying in the Union, we'll go into the next with a clear majority in favour of independence. Expect dirty tricks, underhand dealings, machinations and panicked bribes.

The only proper time for us to have a second referendum is when the opinion polls show that there is a large, clear and consistent majority in favour of Scotland becoming independent. That's the best time for another vote, the only time, a time when the referendum is effectively a formality and will merely be a rubber stamping of what everyone already knows - that a large majority of the Scottish population want independence. A second referendum should be the formalisation of what will by then already be the settled will of the Scottish people for independence.

We can't afford to lose a second independence referendum, because then it really will be off the table for thirty years to come. But the time when there's a large and consistent majority in the polls for independence is also going to be the time when Westminster is least disposed to consent to one, because they'll know they're going to lose. They'll be more embarrassed than a woman who has realised that she's got the same taste in bras as Lord Sewel. This exactly what has been happening in Catalonia, only without the bras.

In Catalonia there's never been much doubt about the outcome of an independence referendum. Opinion polls have consistently shown a large majority in favour of Catalan independence, and consequently the Madrid government has been vehement in its refusal to consent to a referendum.

The time is still not right for a second referendum. Before that happens we need a clear strategy for a Scottish currency, a prospectus that neutralises the economic attacks of the last referendum campaign, and a means of ensuring that the terms of the debate are not set by the London-centric media but by the people of Scotland and a Scottish media which is representative of them. But what we must do in the next Holyrood election is to vote for those parties which unambiguously and clearly spell out in their manifestos that the right to hold a second referendum is in the gift of the Scottish people, not David Cameron.

We are sovereign in this land, not Westminster. Westminster is only our parliament because we currently consent to allow it to be, and we can withdraw that consent at any time we choose. That's the political reality, and politics trumps any legalistic machinations.

David Cameron isn't going to tell me when I can have a say on the future of my country. What Scotland's people decide is not a serving suggestion for Cameron to ignore at his pleasure.

## A Thistle Grows in the Rubble

*30 July 2015*

Back in the 1960s when I was a wean, if you were bright enough you could go to university for free, there was an NHS that was safe and secure, there were nationalised blue trains that were the height of modernity, and when you left school you could get a job for life. My parents enjoyed opportunities that had been denied to their parents.

It wasn't a paradise. It was very far from that. There were evil Tories aplenty, and they enjoyed a significant support in Scotland from the big drum banging brigade. Sectarianism and racism were rampant and socially acceptable, the dread question what school did you go to was asked at job interviews. Homophobia wasn't just commonplace, it was obligatory. But there was a Labour party to act a bulwark, a defence against the worst excesses of the establishment and the bosses. We felt that Labour stood on our side, that we had a powerful ally that could look the establishment in the eye and say No. We felt safe.

People looked down on furren lands with their generals and their coups and their coalition governments that crashed as frequently as a Fiat with no brakes. Scandals and corruption were things that happened in far away places, and we could watch from afar and feel smugly superior. For all its faults, Britain was the gold standard of democracy. Or so we thought.

We were naive, childlike in our trust. We knew nothing of the sex abuse, the cover ups, the corruption and the sleaze. These were things that happened elsewhere, in those foreign lands we were taught to look down on. Not here. We were better than that. We had the British state to save us. We had the safety blanket of social security, and for all the many faults of Britain for the most part we felt safe.

And then came Thatcher, and the British state ate itself. It consumed Scotland and the North to build glittering towers where bankers could worship money. The rich got rich and the poor got kicked in guts that they have nothing to fill. In the towns and cities that formed the powerhouse that drove the Industrial Revolution there were once factories but now there are only food banks. The safety net is a tattered tissue of begrudgement called welfare on which no one fares well, given only to those deemed deserving by the arbitrary tick of a box on a form. We've got a state that offers nothing, but demands ever more, becomes ever more intrusive. It snoops and it pries and demands that we hide nothing from it. But it hides away its own secrets. If you've got nothing to hide you've got nothing to fear, say the powerful people who keep their sins secret with a Jimmy Savile smile. How's about that then.

Britain protects the rich and powerful. It covers up their vile crimes against children. In Britain, protecting the reputations of members of the establishment is more important than the life of your child. Britain robs from the poor to enrich the wealthy. It exists in a network of connection and nods and handshakes and mutual backslapping that exclude the majority. They have power but no accountability. The higher your paygrade, the less likely you are to carry the can. Only the little people have to resign for their failures. This is Britain.

Britain bombs and blasts the fabric of other countries, and calls in the army when the shattered citizens of states Britain has made fail come seeking refuge. Demonising and dehumanising, human suffering becomes a swarm. Compassion is a weakness. Care is privatised. Charity only for a hand-picked few. The only jobs for life are the jobs the rich and powerful give to themselves and their children, while the rest of us scramble for coins in the dust they throw up in their haste to avoid paying tax. We now live in the furren land we once looked down on. This state is alien to the likes of you and me.

And the Tories are still Tories but now Labour has joined them. Evil twin dark stars orbiting around the black hole that swallows all hope, devours all that is good, reduces and shackles all that is progress.

Tony Blair promised to reform the House of Lords, a chamber composed of hereditary peers who had the right to affect our laws because of who their dad was. It was an insult to democracy and had no place in a modern society. True to his word, Tony reformed the Lords. He replaced it with the only thing worse. Tony replaced the lottery of genes and birth order with political patronage, appointees who get their privilege as a reward for services rendered.

Now we have a Labour party whose leading lights struggle with the very concept of democracy. John McTernan, the former spin doctor to Tony Blair, thinks that ordinary party members should do as they're told. They should vote for the candidate that their betters tell them to vote for, and if they don't then the person the little people elect should be summarily evicted from office.

There are those who cling on to past glories and old stories like dried up chewing gum on a broken pavement. What they love is the image of a Britain that never really existed, the surface gloss not the rot underneath. But the truth is that you can't really love something that is kept hidden from you. If you don't know the truth, you live and love in a lie.

And I think of all those who cling on to the comfort blanket of myths and still believe that Scotland shouldn't stand on its own feet. I feel sorry for them, living in the cotton wool of lies. Blind to reality, deaf to truth, living on hopes of change that will never be delivered. The only hope is in our own hands, in the changes we make ourselves. We can be agents of that change. It only takes faith in yourself. Trust yourself, or trust the McTernans of this world. That's the only choice remaining.

Look on the wreckage of the British state. Smell the rot. Inhale the heady gases of decay. Then look to the north and see the green shoots of a thistle, growing and thriving in the rubble.

## A Moan About Useful Idiots

*1 August 2015*

Let's be very clear here, British democracy is a myth. It's as much an invention as the pseudo-mediaeval pageantry of the state opening of parliament, and in fact both inventions date to the same time. British democracy is the democracy of an establishment which has never been successfully challenged, and which maintains its corpse like grasp on the sclerotic organs of state by co-opting useful idiots and spreading its virus of acquisitive greed and self-interest to those who are selfish and egoistic enough to offer up their veins to the vampires of power. Useful idiots like Michelle the Moan. She's being rewarded for her epic trolling during the independence campaign and her services to the Caledonian cringe and filling the pages of the Daily Record with photies of a fake tan.

I did try to be fair. I sat down and carefully thought about what Michelle has achieved, and tried to think of reasons why she should be awarded a peerage and given the right to make laws for the rest of us. I really tried. But I failed utterly, just like the UK fails to represent Scotland. I'm sure Michelle will be happy with her new privileges, and will utterly fail to comprehend why the rest of us are unhappy about it.

Michelle the Moan is going to the House of Lords to sit as a Tory peer, where she'll receive £300 a day for the whingeing and carping she's previously done in return for free publicity. She's sitting as a peer because no one in their right minds would ever vote for her. Her tweets prove that she's semi-literate and has opinions that are normally only seen in the editorial columns of the Daily Mail. Now she's going to the Lords where she can unveil her new range of support products for the manboobs who dominate that place, she's gone to join the useless lumps of fat without any purpose or function.

The peerage has been awarded for Michelle's services to complaining about independence supporters in the pages of the Record. She will at least feel at home in the Lords, she's spent her working life supporting tits and now the tits have returned the favour. This is a woman who thought it entirely appropriate to bug the office of one of her employees, and now she's going to get a say on whether the UK Government can snoop on the rest of us. In theory she could even end up with a cabinet post, as minister of state for whingeing.

The Moan is just one of the new peers. Or as I like to call them, David Cameron has decided that there are too many politicians who can be held to account by the voters, so he's reducing the number of MPs in the Commons. But by way of compensation he's creating a slew of new lardies. It's not just Michelle, he's also giving peerages to a whole bunch of nonentities who just happen to have given the Tory party £23 million in donations. Just one, Michael Farmer, a former Tory treasurer, has personally given £9 million in donations to the Conservative party. British democracy is sold cheaply. It's whored out for a couple of million, a seat on a board of directors, or an expensively paid consultancy. At least in proper dictatorships they don't make any pretence that there's anything honourable in their political appointees.

The new peers are only accountable to Davie and the social pressure of their golf clubs, which makes them a far more efficient means of screwing over the public. Davie's offering peerages to 50 odd useful idiots, some of whom are very odd indeed. In return they get to invent fancy new names for themselves, and our ridiculously deferent media goes along with the charade and uses the made up self-granted titles awarded to Lord Sook Up of Political Donation and Lady Bra-Strap of Unionist Lift But Don't Separate. I won't be using Michelle's silly new title, and I suggest no one else does either. I won't use the silly titles that any of those self-important useful idiots give to themselves. That's the job of the useful idiots of the mainstream media.

Let's be clear here. When we refer to these self-important non-entities by titles awarded by a PM in return for a political donation we are not being polite. We are prostrating ourselves in the dirt and begging to be kicked in the teeth. There are urophiliacs with more self-respect. Referring to an adult as Mr or Ms so and so ought to be perfectly polite enough for anyone. We should not collude in our own humiliation by cooperating with a system which demeans democracy.

But they're not titles, they're not honours. They are badges of shame. Calling yourself a lord or a lady is to make a public statement that you are a leech, a parasite, an anti-democrat. It's saying that you owe your position to patronage, that you are, in fact, a bought person, a slave to the system in a gilded ermine lined cage. It's saying that you sold your principles for £300 per day. It's saying you're cheap, and in doing so you're saying that we are all cheap and worthless and that democracy has no value.

Giving a peerage to a minor businessperson with the opinions of a semi-literate tabloid editorial is the epic trolling of an entire nation, a present to the indy voters of Scotland on JK Rowling's birthday. This is the sort of respect agenda that's supposed to make us want to stay British. I'm not proud to be a citizen of this state, it's an affront to the intelligence of a six year old. The real cringe isn't the Scottish Cringe, it's the British one. Look at the antics of the wildlife killing royals and their welfare payments that run into the millions and we're told to feel proud when we should be feeling angry. From Willnkate down to Michelle the Moan, it's a system based on patronage, privilege and co-opting useful idiots into gushing praise for ludicrous leeches. And it treats us like idiots who can be disposed of once we are no longer useful.

Being British is an embarrassment and the sooner we escape this ridiculous Ruritanian charade, the better we'll all be. The likes of Michelle are no bloody use to us.

## Fantasy League Politics

*4 August 2015*

It's a hard life being the leading candidate for branch office manager of the Labour party in Scotland. How exactly do you make a convincing and principled pitch for a job where the main requirement is that the post holder has neither convictions nor principles. It's one of those philosophical paradoxes that would exercise a great intellect, only the job also means surrendering anything approaching intelligence, or indeed even common sense.

This week leading candidate Kezia has written an article for the Guardian spelling out her dream of abolishing the House of Lords and replacing it with an elected chamber which meets in Glasgow. This will piss off Michelle the Moan no end, as it will seriously impair her ability to take selfies on her veranda with a view of Tower Bridge. Selfies with a view of Greggs in Shettleston just don't have quite the same social cachet. Although you can at least get a yum yum, which adds considerably more to the sum total of human happiness than anything Michelle has ever done. Logically then, the benches of the Lords should not be full of opinionated minor businesspersons who sook up to the Tories, but coconut buns and bread rolls. But the Lords went stale a long time ago.

Kezia thinks that her great idea will bring massive new job opportunities to Glasgow. Sex workers, bra suppliers, drug dealers and purveyors of brown envelopes would all see booming trade. Although to be fair, Glesca cooncil has already being doing sterling work in that department for years.

Sadly however, Kezia's great idea has about as much chance of happening as Gordon Matheson getting through a car park without a twinge of embarrassment - or introducing the long promised city wide free Wi-Fi in time for the next election, seeing as how they didn't manage it in time for the last. But then Kezia is merely continuing in the traditions of the Labour party in making promises that have no chance of ever seeing life outside the invisible jam jar.

Labour promised to abolish the House of Lords in its very first manifesto over 100 years ago. It took the party until 1997 to introduce legislation to reform the Lords - not to abolish it mind. Despite the crushing majority enjoyed by Tony Blair and the all singing all dancing promises that things could only get better, Labour replaced the unfair hereditary system with the only system that could be even less fair. Blair gave us a bloated upper chamber stuffed full of political placepersons, timeservers, party donors, and people who were being rewarded for services rendered to political parties, all of whom were appointed for life. There are actually dictatorships which have more of a fig leaf of democratic accountability than this.

So Kezia can make fine promises about reforming the Lords which have the same political validity as daydreaming about what you'll spend the millions on once you win the Euromillions lottery. You have about the same chance as winning the Euromillions jackpot as you do being struck by a meteorite, which makes both vastly more likely than the Labour party actually fulfilling its promises. Not that you'd know any of this from watching BBC Scotland, which is still fixated on NHS waiting times and calling for Nicola Sturgeon to apologise. Labour doing what it was set up to do over 100 years ago is as likely as BBC Scotland producing a news and current affairs programme that people actually want to watch.

Kezia's making her big plans because Labour in Scotland has no plans. Neither Kezia nor the second runner wossiface want Labour in Scotland to become a real Scottish Labour party, neither will commit to the abolition of Trident, neither will say anything which contradicts the drones and automatons who run the party from London. Hope springs eternal, but not in the Labour party in Scotland, where only dopes spring eternal. All we get is the whoosh of the vacuum, filled only with grandiose ideas that will never come to pass and the constantly repeated mantra of SNP Bad.

After all, being Labour branch office manager in Scotland means that you have a boss whose job is defined by vacuity. With the exception of Jeremy Corbyn who is attracting so much opprobrium you'd think he was in the SNP, none of the leadership contenders want to say anything that's remotely controversial, or which even has any content. This is most clearly illustrated by Liz Kendall, who is clearly going for a Barbie airhead approach to politics. This may be a post-modern feminist statement, but it's really just more likely that she's terrified of saying anything that a Tory newspaper might find remotely contentious.

Liz has published a wee list of key aims for her leadership bid, aspirations which could easily be confused with the gushing breathy dreams of a contestant for Miss World. Liz wants to share power with the people, build a more caring society, and ensure a future of hope for our young people. None of this actually means anything, and it is as bereft of semantic content as Kezia's aspirations for a Hoose of Lairds in Glesca are bereft of any connection to reality. That's all we can expect in modern Britain, austerity, crap wages and working conditions, the demonisation of the poor and the marginalised, and happy clappy sound bites from politicians who wrap themselves in a flag while denying that they're British nationalists.

But Liz is a well-rounded leader to be, she also wants a national day of niceness every day, a wishing tree in every constituency office, blue skies in August, and little birds which sing in every branch twittering happiness as the little people skip gaily to their minimum wage jobs on zero hours contracts. Only this being Labour they'll be little birds which sing and report back to Liz so that she can keep tabs on everyone. The Labour right being noted for its authoritarian tendencies. Liz wants a future where disabled and unemployed people are drowned in a vat of paperwork by smiling and caring people who are doing it for their own good.

Welcome to Britain 2015, going backwards not forwards, but we're doing it with a happy soundbite and fantasy league politics. Don't you feel proud?

# Signs of Repayment of a Debt to Gaelic and Scots

*6 August 2015*

Muriel Gray is such a wag, sending witty Tweets about railway station name signs which are bilingual in English and Gaelic. Well I say witty. It's witty in the same way that Adam Sandler is a comedian, or deep fried Mars bars with a Buckie chaser aren't a stereotype. I hesitate to repeat it in case you fall about laughing so much you hit your head on the coffee table and kill yourself, but Muriel said that the biggest social problem in Scotland used to be lost Gaelic speakers begging to know where they were, but now with bilingual railway signs we have so sorted that one. I know, right. Laugh? I nearly contributed to the School of Art restoration fund.

Muriel's unfunny wee jokette with its redolence of cultural cringe might have been just an off the cuff remark, but it taps into the arrogance of the Scottish British establishment. Scottish culture only has value or worth when it's a particular kind of Scottish culture, preferably the kind that can be used to impress ironic beards in cereal cafés in Shoreditch, or sold as conceptual art for an inflated price tag to a rich collector. When it can be monetised, in other words.

But Gaelic is a dead language, protest people who are determined to kill it off. Gaelic is not dead. It still has speakers, but it would seem that there are people in Scotland who really ought to know better - self-described political or cultural commentators - who insist that it's dead and we should just pull the plug on the life support machine. Some people really need to reflect on the meaning of the term 'self-fulfilling prophecy'. And while they're at it they should ponder the amount of time, energy and money that the British state has put into killing the other languages of these islands.

Scotland would not exist without Gaelic or Scots. The languages made this country what it is, Gaelic brought Scotland into existence, Scots was the language of the Scottish state. They made us who we are, and they are proper to Scotland and nowhere else. Only Scotland can save them. A vast amount of Scottish literature and writing was composed in Gaelic and Scots, and if we lose the languages we lose that part of ourselves. Gaelic and Scots form the roots of the Scottish tree, without them the tree dies and we become a parasitical culture.

Imagine there was a harmless cute and fluffy wee animal which now only lived in a small part of Scotland but which was once widespread throughout the country. No one would object to government money being used to save the creature. No one would object to initiatives to restore it to parts of its former range. People like those who inhabit Schools of Art would front impassioned appeals to save this vital part of Scottish natural diversity which has shaped our landscapes and informed our mythology. Scottish languages are a part of natural diversity too. If we don't protect them, they'll die. And we will be the generation that killed them.

Then there are those who indulge in whataboutery. What about Pictish eh? What about the language of the Cumbric Britons. Are they not Scottish languages too? Why should we not try to revive them as well as Gaelic and Scots? But we're not comparing like with like here. Gaelic and Scots are living languages. They still have speakers, they are fully attested. Pictish and Cumbric are fossil languages, surviving only in place and personal names and a handful of words in ancient texts and inscriptions. Not enough of them survives to attempt to revive them. It would be like trying to revive a long extinct creature from a few scraps of bone. Gaelic and Scots still live and breathe despite the best efforts of too many in Scotland to kill them off, or allow them to die of neglect.

Often the people who insist that Gaelic is dead and of no relevance to modern Scotland regard themselves as socialists or social democrats. Yes, Labour supporters, we're looking at you. It's ironic then that a person who believes that the role of the state is to intervene in the workings of the free market to ameliorate its negative effects on society believe so strongly in an entirely mythical free market of languages.

There's no such thing as a free market in languages. No one wakes up one morning and decides, today I'm going to transfer my linguistic allegiance to Classical Nahuatl and do my shopping in Morrison's just like an ancient Aztec. Although to be fair the ritual sacrifice of check out staff is frowned upon nowadays. The truth is there is no free choice in language use, the language you use is determined by politics and power. Gaelic has been marginalised and driven to the verge of extinction because of politics and power, not because Scottish people made a free and unforced choice to give it up in favour of English. The same holds true for Lowland Scots.

The attitude is that the Gaelic language isn't like a Charles Rennie Mackintosh masterpiece, it doesn't bring in the tourists, and so has no value and it's a waste to spend public money on it. Public money should of course be spent on restoring the School of Art - and it should be spent on protecting and fostering the Gaelic language as well. Both are equally artefacts of Scottish culture.

The purpose of Gaelic signage is to give the language a public presence. Gaelic was once the dominant language of all of Scotland north and west of a line drawn roughly from Gretna to Musselburgh, and was even found in the far south east as well. Gaelic signs remind us all that the English language has never been the only language of Scotland, and make a public statement that the language enjoys respect and support. That's why they're there, to remind English speaking Scots that their lazy assumption of English language dominance can and should be challenged, and that's why members of the Scottish political and cultural establishment object to them.

But more than that, Gaelic and Scots have been marginalised because of the actions of the state, so the state has a duty to ensure that the languages survive.

That's moral restitution, it's the repayment of a debt. We owe it to our languages, we owe it to ourselves.

## Ken's Reactionary Cringe

*8 August 2015*

Ken Macintosh, the not leading candidate for branch manager of the Labour party in Scotland - who is better known as "Who's he?" even in his own party - has stated that Scotland shouldn't get any more powers from Westminster. Ken's really keen to attract back the voters that Labour has lost to the SNP, and thinks that the best way to do it is to refuse to concede any more devolution at all. Labour calls itself the party of devolution, Ken calls it the party of you'll have had your devolution.

Ken is concerned that a woman whose only ability is to shoehorn an attack on the SNP into every single statement has greater public recognition than he does. Just this week alone, Kezia Dugdale has blamed the SNP for letting her tea go cold, demanded the resignation of Nicola Sturgeon after a wean in her local swing park bruised his knee, and written an impassioned article for the Labour supporting Daily Mail bewailing the fact that SNP supporters laugh at her. Faced with such determined opposition, and let's face it it's the only opposition Labour is capable of mounting, Ken decided he had to do something. He looked around for a likely bandwagon and jumped on it. I'm just like Jeremy Corbyn! cried Ken, except for the socialism, the opposition to nuclear weapons, and the desire to renationalise privatised industries and utilities that is. So failing the possession of any traditional socialist policies, and in order to show that he's a traditional Labour politician in tune with Old Labour in Scotland, Ken decided to do the traditional Labour in Scotland thing, and to tell a load of auld mince to the media.

Ken gave the interview in order to raise his profile, because at the moment he's not even the best known person inside his own head. So brave Ken set out to court the Yes leaning populace, and told Commonspace, a pro-independence news site, that he doesn't want Scotland to get any devolution pudding, because we still haven't digested the stale kale and rotten potatoes of the Smith Commish. He did also manage to get some attacks on the SNP into the piece, but no one really noticed because Labour attacks on the SNP are like bad smells, after a while your nose grows accustomed to them and you no longer notice.

In fact, Ken's pretty uncomfortable with the powers that Scotland currently has. This is because in the mental universe of Who's He, Scots are a backward looking atavistic bunch of bigots, religious fundamentalists, right wing extremists, and Ruth Davidsons. The most popular car in Scotland is a tank, and they cause havoc on the M8 every rush hour as they compete to run over migrants and gay people. The favourite pastime of a Scottish person is dressing up like John Knox and going out on the town looking for a witch to burn, but not on the Sabbath. On the Sabbath we go around in massed groups looking for budgies' swings to tie up. But then someone pointed out that that constituted work and was sinful, and so we had to take turns throwing rocks at one another. It's a damned hard life being a puritan bigot you know. But looking on the bright side, we are apparently very good at it, according to Ken. In fact, according to Ken it's about the only thing we're any good at. I'd better not say any more about how good we are at bigoted intolerance though, because vanity is a sin and someone might throw a rock at me.

But back to the man who makes Iain Gray seem high profile and James Kelly seem likeable. Why, said Who's He, if Scotland gets more powers from Westminster in 20 years' time Scots might elect a right wing reactionary government, and that would never do. It's the duty of the Labour party to protect Scotland from reactionary right wingery by, for example, not voting against Tory cuts to social security and adopting Conservative policies wholesale in order to make a pleading pitch to the strivey achievey people who make up focus groups. Ken thinks it's far safer for Scots to leave all the really important heavy lifting powers of government in the hands of a parliament most of whose representatives are right wing reactionary extremists right now, and who look set to remain so after the next General Election in 2020.

Anyway, the logic, such as it is, is that Scotland is inhabited by reactionary provincials, and we rely upon the good graces of the Westminster Parliament to teach us how to act like civilised human beings. We needed Westminster to introduce anti-racist legislation, equal wage laws for women, and gay rights, because Scotland would have been incapable of working out for itself that

319

it's wrong to discriminate. Scotland isn't a major multicultural centre like London, and we live in a cave with a brown paper bag over our heads, pining for the days when the Calvinists banned Sunday shopping.

Saying that Scotland can't be trusted with the levers of power is hardly a positive selling point for a man who aspires to be First Minister. It's like giving your car keys to a man who tells you that he's only capable of driving sheep - although to be fair that's quite a good qualification for a Labour party parliamentary leader. But amongst the voting public, "Vote for me because your country is mediocre and I'm the best person to manage its mediocrity," isn't what you might call a strong selling point.

Poor Who's He, he's got a very bad case of the Cringe, and the fact that Cringeworthiness is considered a positive in a serious contender for leader of a major political party is a sad illustration of the extent to which Labour, and the Union in general, has lost its way. So now we know that we're really better together because we're socially inadequate - like those poor lonely souls on Channel 4 dating shows who can't get laid. Vote for me, says Ken, because you're ugly, you're inadequate, and you can't get a shag. Ken's Cringe tells us that there's nothing that the Union has left to offer Scotland, and that we're far better off without it.

## The Price of Failure

*10 August 2015*

**W**hat's the price of failure? If you fail in your marriage your significant other will become significant in a divorce courty sort of way. If you fail to impress in a job interview, you'll find yourself having to impress in a job centre interview. And if you're a Westminster politician who fails at their job you'll get handed a nice title and a made up name and very often a job for life too. The UK dishonours system is proof that British governments are the only organisms which rot from the top down.

Having wowed us with Lady McMoan and her peerage for Unionist Trolling during the independence referendum, it has now transpired that a number of political losers, has-beens, and also rans are to be rewarded for their failure. The good voters of Inverness and surrounding districts might have thought that by deserting Danny Alexander en masse so he ended up in a poor third place in what had formerly been a stronghold for his party, that they were giving him such a showing up that he'd crawl under a rock and never dare to show his face again. But think again minions, Danny is getting a knighthood for services to Tory toadying and gleeful austeritising. All we need now is for Magrit Curran to be made a Dame for the pantomime to be complete.

Only no one shouts out "they're behind you" to the Labour party in Scotland since they're the ones in last place.

To be fair, much as we all enjoy castigating the one who is a disgrace to ginger haired-ness everywhere, Danny didn't single-handedly destroy the Lib Dems as a credible political force. He had help. Help like Menzies Campbell who decided not to stand as an MP in May partly on the grounds that he's older than the democratic franchise, but mainly because he knew he was going to get gubbed.

And gubbed is precisely what happened to the Lib Dems in the Mingin one's old seat. But never fear, we've now got Lord Mingin of Fife to help protect the establishment against democracy and from the choices expressed by the likes of you and me in the ballot box. He's looking forward to speaking in the House of Lords and regaling them with tales of when he found out that fire had been invented. He plans to use this exciting new invention to burn down any chance of home rule for Scotland.

None of this should come as any surprise. The British establishment always rewards its own failures. Back in the 1990s Michael Forsyth was leader of the Scottish Tories and presided over that party's annihilation. During the 1997 General Election the voters of Scotland said in no uncertain terms that we didn't want Michael, we didn't want his party, and we didn't want his party's policies. The Tories lost every single seat.

This is failure of a truly abject variety. You can't do any worse at your job. If he was a teacher he'd have been subject to a banning order and would not be allowed within 200 metres of a school. If he was a doctor he'd have been struck off and wouldn't even be allowed to sell bottles of vitamins and healing crystals. But he's a politician so Michael was rewarded with a seat in the Lords where he still casts his malign influence on Scottish public life and affects our laws and legislation.

Where there are no consequences for failure then there is no incentive to do a good job. All there is is an incentive to line one's own pockets, to climb the greasy career pole, or please the powerful who hand out rewards and directorships like dog chews to the good boys and girls who beg nicely, give a paw, and snarl and bark at the proles.

It's not just the lamentable Lib Dems who have been rewarded for their inadequacies. We're also getting Lord Darling of Naw Ye Cannae. Just when you thought that you'd never have to listen to one of his blinking expositions ever again, he's coming back for a sequel. This time with ermine. Ali's still smarting that Gordie Broon took the credit for saving the Union, but relieved that it's likewise Gordie who's coping the blame for the Vow that failed to wow. Gordie isn't getting a peerage, but only because no one knows where he's hiding. There's another failure that no one responsible is paying the price for, it's the people of Scotland who are copping it.

Scotland's voters signalled their displeasure at the General Election in May by pandificating all the Unionist parties. Since receiving that almighty kick in the nads, the Unionist parties have displayed no sign that the pain signals have connected with anything approaching a higher brain function. They continue to act precisely as they did before, ignoring the democratically expressed will of the Scottish people and rewarding themselves for their failure. We can only conclude that they do not possess any conscious awareness and are in fact brain dead. All that is left is to demolish what little is remaining and pour electoral paraquat over the smouldering ruins. If they are incapable of learning the lesson of failure, all we can do is to cut them out of the game.

In the latest opinion poll of voting intentions for Holyrood next year, it looks as though that's exactly what Scotland is going to do. Gobsmackingly, the SNP is on 62%. The SNP and the Greens could between them take well over 80 of the seats in the Scottish Parliament. Labour is set to lose all its constituency seats. The new leader's great idea is to bound over the deep chasm facing the party in two leaps. The Tories remain in the slough of Scottish irrelevance to which they were consigned by Michael Forsyth. Meanwhile it's entirely possible that the Lib Dems will be wiped out in Scotland and Wullie Rennie will go back to driving the bus to Kelty.

Phase one is almost complete: removing the parties of the Union from Scottish politics. Phase two will soon begin: removing Scottish politics from the Union. That will be the real price of Westminster failure.